National
Monuments
Record of
Scotland
Jubilee

A Guide
to the
Collections

Royal
Commission on the
Ancient and
Historical
Monuments of
Scotland

NATIONAL MONUMENTS RECORD OF SCOTLAND JUBILEE

·

A GUIDE TO THE COLLECTIONS

N·M·R·S 1941 1991

EDINBURGH: HMSO

PENNYCUICK HOUSE EDINBURGHSHIRE.   CRAIG CROOKE CASTLE EDINBURGHSHIRE   HOPETOUN HOUSE LINLITHGOWSHIRE

The Royal Commission on the Ancient and
Historical Monuments of Scotland

Commissioners

The Right Honourable The Earl of Crawford
and Balcarres (*Chairman*)
Professor Leslie Alcock, MA, FSA, FRHistS
Professor R J Cramp, CBE, MA, BLitt, FSA
The Honourable Lord Cullen
Professor J D Dunbar-Nasmith, CBE, BA,
RIBA, PPRIAS
Professor A A M Duncan, MA, FBA
Mrs P E Durham
Dr Deborah Howard, MA, PhD, FSA
The Honourable Peregrine D E M Moncrieffe
Professor T C Smout, MA, PhD

Secretary
R J Mercer, Esq, MA, FSA

To the Memory of
Colin E McWilliam
Director, Scottish National Buildings Record
1951–1957

© Crown copyright 1991
First published 1991

ISBN 0 11 494125 4

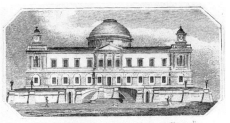

Miniature engraved vignettes c.1810

CONTENTS

PREFACE

This Guide is published to mark the Jubilee of the National Monuments Record of Scotland, an event which is also being signalled by an exhibition. Fifty years ago, in 1941, its precursor, the Scottish National Buildings Record, was founded. In their Introduction Ian Gow and Graham Ritchie tell a fascinating story of an almost incongruous birth in the violent and austere days of the Second World War. They tell of the growth of the Record, leading to the vigorously active state of the collection and data-base today. This large and composite national archive of Scotland's archaeological sites and historic buildings is of a kind which is unique in Britain. It ranges from late seventeenth-century manuscripts and original design drawings by most of Scotland's leading architects to work of more recent times, including archaeological excavation- and survey-reports.

The catalogue, which forms the bulk of the following text, is the beginning of a process which will take many years to accomplish. It does not include the very considerable holdings of the NMRS Library, and it cannot cover the mass of holdings of the collections that emanate from the field investigations of the Royal Commission (RCAHMS) itself. It does, however, provide a cumulative list of the historical and deposited collections that add so much zest to the content of the Record.

Finally, any introduction to a catalogue and exhibition that celebrate fifty years of achievement in the Record in Scotland must include mention of the name of Kitty Cruft, who moves into, no doubt busy, retirement as the Exhibition opens. The wit, erudition, dedication and leadership of Miss Cruft have served and inspired generations of architectural historians working in Scotland. She will be sorely missed, and the Record, as it continues to grow and expand its scope, will bear witness to her achievements.

CRAWFORD AND BALCARRES

Editorial Notes and Acknowledgements

The alphabetically-arranged list of entries which forms the main text of this publication was compiled from catalogue-slips relating to the historical and other deposited collections in the NMRS. Each entry begins with the title of the collection (usually appearing as the location which is the main subject, or provenance, of the collection, or occasionally with the architect or originator of the subjects described therein); there follows a brief description of the collection's contents, in some cases accompanied by summary biographical or contextual notes; the final element, printed in italics, indicates, as appropriate, the date and source of acquisition, or copying, together with details of the NMRS accession number or Society of Antiquaries of Scotland MS number. The reader is asked to note particularly that the appearance of a location in this catalogue does not in any way imply that all the Record material relevant to the location is listed here; conversely, the absence of any location from the catalogue does not necessarily signify the lack of evidence relating to it elsewhere in the Record.

For the production of this book the Commission is indebted to many people, a special word of thanks for outside assistance being due to Mr Maurice Brown, Professor Alistair Rowan and Dr David Walker, who contributed to the Introduction; and to Mrs Jill Lever and Dr Howard Colvin, whose advice was invaluable in formulating the entries in the catalogue. Commission staff involved in the work included Ian Gow and Graham Ritchie, who wrote the Introduction, with editorial assistance from Kitty Cruft, Gordon Maxwell and Roger Mercer. The compilation of the Catalogue was carried out by Ian Gow, with the assistance of Lesley Ferguson and Diana Murray; the ordering and presentation of the text for publication was largely supervised by John Stevenson, who shared with Ian Scott in the design and layout of the catalogue; Anne Martin and Robert Adam were responsible for the photographic material used for illustrating the volume. For the typing a special word of thanks is due to Christine Allan and Carole Buglass.

INTRODUCTION

In 1991 the National Monuments Record of Scotland will celebrate its Jubilee as successor to the Scottish National Buildings Record, founded on 19 May 1941. The year, perhaps, gives a clue to its original grim purpose. It was set up during the Second World War to make an emergency record of Scotland's historic architecture in anticipation of its possible destruction through enemy action. The Scottish body was the counterpart of the National Buildings Record in London, but, while they embraced the same ideals, the former inevitably took on a local colouring.

The history of the London Record, founded in February 1941, is a remarkable story of private initiative on the part of England's architects and has been recounted elsewhere by Stephen Croad.[1] In their initial enthusiasm, it was intended that the Record should cover not only England and Wales, but also Scotland. However, the difficulties in raising private funds to augment the slender grant which was all the Treasury could spare in wartime, meant that it soon became obvious that they could not hope to tackle Scotland. Lord Reith, the Minister of Works, who had been instrumental in gaining governmental support for the scheme, being a Scot, was naturally anxious to secure equivalent coverage for Scotland, the more so, because her industrial heartlands and fragile communications carried across bridges made her a prime target. A letter from the Saltire Society in March 1941 helped to stir the Edinburgh branch of the Ministry of Works into activity.

Although the government was determined that the Scottish body should be independent and distanced from the Ministry of Works, it was realised that the foundation of the Edinburgh Record might require more direct encouragement than that in London, which had been swept along on a tide of enthusiasm by the Royal Institute of British Architects. It was initially felt that the functions might be carried out by the Royal Commission on the Ancient and Historical Monuments of Scotland. However, this body's much reduced

wartime establishment made such a solution impracticable (although, of course, this was to be the eventual outcome).

The first step in the creation of the new body was the appointment of a suitable Chairman. The Marquess of Bute was the unanimous choice of Lord Reith's advisers, because both the Marquess and his father had an outstanding record in preserving Scotland's historic buildings. It was also hoped, in view of the shortage of funds, that the Marquess might give financial support to the venture. Lord Reith soon discovered that Lord Bute had no intention of being merely a figurehead, as he was a seasoned campaigner in the cause of Scotland's historic architecture. Whereas his father, the third Marquess, had devoted much energy to saving individual outstanding medieval buildings, Lord Bute had been an important pioneer in his appreciation of the architectural value that groups of relatively modest buildings can provide. In spite of their historic interest, these houses were all too often threatened with destruction because they did not meet current housing standards, and Lord Bute was impatient with the attitude of the Scottish Local Authorities who lacked the imagination to realise that, for a relatively modest outlay, such houses could be retained and brought up to standard. Incensed by a spate of demolitions in Fife, Lord Bute established 'The Friends of Falkland' to front his purchase of many threatened buildings in that historic Royal Burgh.

Lord Reith doubtless hoped that Lord Bute would have been delighted to accept the Chairmanship of a body with interests so attuned to his own. He must therefore have been acutely disappointed by Bute's reply, which stated that he saw little point in the proposed Record unless it had powers to protect historic buildings akin to the existing scheduling of Ancient Monuments, and that the average Scottish Local Authority posed a no less serious threat to ancient buildings than the *Luftwaffe*. The Marquess also singled out the existing legislation in Scotland, which encouraged owners of unoccupied historic houses to remove the roofs in order to avoid paying rates. In spite of attempts to mollify him, the Marquess responded with named examples of exactly the kind of destruction

that he deplored and went so far as to suggest that the Record, in pin-pointing the existence of historic buildings, might serve only to hasten their destruction by Local Authorities. The civil servants in Edinburgh began to search about for a more compliant candidate, until matters were smoothed over through Lord Reith's diplomacy and a reminder of the urgency of the task. Lord Bute, with the assistance of Reginald Fairlie, his consultant architect, drew up a list of members of the proposed Scottish Council who were to direct the National Buildings Record's work. The list of names, with their attached comments, demonstrates the range of interests that they hoped to harness and shows the geographical spread of representation which they sought:

'*List of Proposed Members of National Buildings Records Council*

Lord Hamilton of Dalzell. Chairman of the Royal Fine Arts Commission.
R Fairlie Esq., Architect. Member of the Ancient Monuments Board and the Ancient Monuments Commission.
D Baird Smith Esq., LL D. President of the Scottish Text Society, Glasgow (who could represent the West side of the country).
Stanley Cursiter Esq., OBE. Director of the National Gallery, Edinburgh.
F C Mears Esq., Architect (who has done a good deal of reconstruction work and town planning).
W N Mackenzie Esq., D Litt. Lecturer in Scottish History, University of Edinburgh.
T F MacLellan Esq. President of the Royal Incorporation of Scottish Architects (who some years ago took much interest in the National Art Survey).
T Innes of Learney, Albany Herald (who comes from Aberdeen and would be a link with the North).
I G Lindsay Esq., Architect. Member of the Ancient Monuments Board (who has done much work privately in the collation of plans and drawings of period houses).
James S Richardson Esq. Inspector of Ancient Monuments (he is the nominee of the Ministry of Works).'

Although Ian Lindsay had already been called up into the Royal Engineers and was thus barred from active involvement, Lord Bute was particularly keen to secure his appointment, in view of his unrivalled experience, gained through drawing up lists of historic buildings in Scottish towns prior to the war.

Lord Bute introduced the inaugural meeting, held in the Caledonian Hotel, Edinburgh, on 19 May 1941, by stating that:

'He had received an invitation from Lord Reith, Minister of Works and Buildings, to form a National Buildings Record Council in Scotland for the purpose of establishing a register of buildings of merit illustrated by drawings and photographs. It was hoped that a Treasury grant might be forthcoming as in England but the amount was not yet known.'

Characteristically, the statement contained no explicit reference to the war. It was also a measure of the widespread threat to Scottish architecture that the Marquess had asked for an immediate lump sum of £5,000, instead of an annual small sum. As this was over twice the sum allowed for London, the £750 yearly payment eventually set was realistic. The Council went on to draw up an action list:

'Dr Baird Smith suggested that in view of recent attacks the western district should receive early attention. In the East, in addition to the Forth coastal towns, Haddington and St Andrews were cited as of special interest.'

This targeting was further refined at a second meeting a month later, the burden of the actual survey work falling upon architectural students. Edinburgh College of Art offered their senior students to the Record during the summer vacation if their expenses were met, and it was resolved to suggest to the College that:

'three students be allocated to Stirling, three to Haddington, three to Edinburgh and six to make drawings and specifications of the bridges over the Tweed and its tributaries.'

One of these students, Maurice Brown, recalled in 1990:

'During the summer of 1940 our whole world had fallen apart. It had taken the German forces barely six weeks to sweep

through the Low Countries, devastate Rotterdam, subdue France and poise themselves on the Channel coast for the invasion of Britain. Defence, of course, was the priority, but with it came a threat to our architectural heritage. In 1941 responsible authorities approached John Walkden, acting head of the School of Architecture, Edinburgh College of Art, for help in compiling a record, at least, of what might not be saved. He quickly got in touch with a number of recent graduates and other students who had dispersed at the end of the academic year and who were still waiting to take up war service. We assembled in Edinburgh on 22 July and by mid-day I was off to Stirling in a party of five with identity passes saying that we were "deputed to measure and sketch the North side of Broad Street and Darnley's House, Stirling, for official record", adding that the work was being done with the knowledge of the military and police authorities and requesting that all possible facilities should be given for the work. Thenceforth our numbers were depleted one by one as call-up papers came through. Early in September only three of us were left. We took our notes and drawings back to Edinburgh and did some further work until I was called up to Devizes in October. Their completion then passed into other hands.'

The work of the Record proceeded on three fronts: the preparation of measured survey drawings, the collation of existing survey records, and photography. Although the Council regarded the first activity as primary, it was realised that the draughtsmen's time must not be wasted in duplicating earlier efforts. Ironically, even if the Record had enjoyed greater financial resources, it would have been unable in wartime to find draughtsmen to employ, as even the students began to be absorbed into the forces. However, the architectural students of the 1930s were generous in presenting relevant measured drawings, prepared as part of their course, or permitting their surveys to be traced. Moreover the upheaval of war had brought a large number of Polish soldiers to Scotland, and, realising that a few of their officers had been trained as architects, Reginald Fairlie had the inspiration to seek

permission for them to be attached to the Record. If they perhaps imported an element of nostalgia for their native architecture to their record drawings of Scotland's historic buildings, the Poles nevertheless produced work of an exceptionally high standard, and one of their number, Stanislaw Tyrowicz, was to become the Record's full-time draughtsman by the end of the war.

Pen tracings were the standard form of record drawing, and it was soon realised that their preservation was of the utmost importance. For this purpose, Lord Bute was able to offer the modern strongroom at Dumfries House, one of his seats; prints were taken from the drawings before they were despatched to the country.

To stimulate interest in the work of the Record, two exhibitions were held. The first, in July 1943, took place in the emptied National Gallery of Scotland and was organised by the Director, Stanley Cursiter. The second took place nine months later, in Glasgow Art Gallery, under the supervision of the Council's local member, Dr Baird Smith. On both occasions the original drawings were regarded as too valuable to exhibit, but, for Glasgow, some of the prints were realistically coloured in gouache. For the latter exhibition the Secretary, George Scott Moncrieff, produced a pamphlet entitled *The Buildings of Scotland*, and James Richardson drew the sketch for its cover. The text reveals a great deal about the Record's aims:

'The choice of subject has not been regulated by the size or importance of a building. The Council has kept in mind the need for a comprehensive central library of architectural drawings, paying considerable attention to those more modest homes of the people which make our villages and smaller buildings so delightful and which should serve to influence the architects who are to build the Scottish communities of the future.'

The compilation of the register of existing drawings was found to be a more difficult task than anticipated, but the production of such a register was the only means to avoid duplication of effort. A list of the most important modern buildings in Edinburgh was

Prestonfield House, Edinburgh; section by
Nicholas Jankowski 1943 for SNBR

compiled and an effort made to match them to surviving drawings. The response to circulars from architectural practices was disappointing, however, the only reply being from Wilson Paterson, who offered prints of the 'Savings Bank in Frederick Street', and the exercise seems to have been dogged by concern about the 'merit' of some of the buildings on the list. A satisfactory register was eventually completed by the octogenarian retired architect, Henry F Kerr.

The Council also attracted gifts of historic drawings for their growing collection. Although they rejected a set of stained glass cartoons as unsuitable, it is very much to their credit that they selected a number of exhibition drawings from the collection of the architect David Bryce (1803–1876), the leading exponent of the Baronial revival in Victorian Scotland, when his collection was offered in

September 1942. The acquisition of measured drawings by James Gillespie provided a link with the earlier recording activities of Sir Rowand Anderson (1834–1921), who had founded the 'National Art Survey of Scotland' in 1895, as part of the teaching method of his Edinburgh School of Applied Art. Gillespie had been one of the bursars appointed to prepare measured surveys of Scotland's historic architecture in accordance with Anderson's programme of instilling the students with a Scottish idiom of design. During the 1920s a part of this collection of 1,500 drawings had been published, and the Council may not have realised that the original designs were stored in the National Portrait Gallery. When Anderson despaired of them being published during his lifetime, he had encouraged James Gillespie to prepare his *Details of Scottish Domestic Architecture* in 1922, and it was the finished drawings for the plates that now entered the Record's collection.

If both modern surveys and old plans rapidly accrued to the Record, photography was perhaps the least successful area of the operations. As in the London Record, there was a strong prejudice against snap-shots. The Record was not well enough off to commission professional photographs, although it did make copies, where possible, from existing negatives, and Ian Lindsay offered to have his collection duplicated. Advice was also sought from the Royal Commission on the Ancient and Historical Monuments of Scotland, whose Secretary, Angus Graham, would have been very surprised to know that he was recognised as something more than an amateur photographer. The Commission had found that photography was most useful for recording details of buildings, and this possibly reinforced the Council's prejudice in favour of measured drawings showing the entire structure.

On the other hand, the value of existing early architectural photographs, with their clarity of detail, was fully realised, and many of the finest historic photographs in the collection, including the set of prints of Melrose Abbey, attributed to Clark, and the prints and paper negatives of John Forbes White, were subsequently purchased from the Edinburgh Photographic Society as a result of contacts established at this time. The Society itself had more than a little experience of architectural survey through their pioneering record of South Edinburgh, compiled between 1911 and 1914; a set of prints deriving from this survey was also acquired by the Record.

Looking through the Buildings Record's Minutes, it is difficult not to feel that the prolonged illness of the Marquess of Bute from 1943 resulted in a loss of impetus, because he had taken such a personal interest in its affairs. Perhaps, too, the initial flurry of activity fell away because much of Scotland remained relatively unscathed by bombing raids. The Council meetings, which had been held monthly in 1941, became quarterly and then erratic.

With the end of the war, the Council dutifully discussed the possibility of publishing the drawings as a fitting conclusion to their labours. In practice, however, there was to be no question of the Record being wound up. It was soon realised that the Record's function was still necessary, although the real debate took place in London, with the fate of the Scottish Record being carried along in its wake. Indeed, Lord Bute had never seen the Record's work as being solely war-related, and even during the height of the bombing in London, records had been made as much to contribute to the 'artistic annals of our country' as to provide practical assistance in the creation of post-war replicas. The end of the war was, in any case, thought to herald a boom in reconstruction, during which the necessity for architectural records would be no less important.

In Scotland the Record also owed its survival to a number of local factors. It was schooled in the art of existing on a shoe-string budget because it had been born in austerity. Because most of its Council were representative, they could be easily replaced when age caught up with them. When the Secretary, George Scott Moncrieff, resigned in July 1945, Haswell Miller (1887–1979), the Keeper of the Scottish National Portrait Gallery, was appointed as a stop-gap solution for six months. He was, in fact, to serve as Secretary for seven years, as this term was successively extended. Under Haswell Miller, the Record enjoyed free accommodation in the Scottish National Portrait Gallery, and Miller was to make two important contributions to the development of the Record. His first achievement was the establishment of a purchase grant, as a result of his memorandum of 23 November 1945. Through this initiative, the rate of accessions accelerated, and books, prints and photographs flowed in. Some of these acquisitions were a result of the Record's existing contacts, like the purchase of Henry Kerr's library and sketchbooks in 1946, while others resulted from Miller's Gallery connections. His most important purchase was the collection of drawings which originated from the sale of part of the Bute collection in 1952, and these drawings by Slezer and others remain the finest of the few seventeenth-century drawings now in the collections.

Sadly the Marquess of Bute's illness was to be a prolonged one, and his resignation was accepted with the greatest reluctance in February 1947. Although it was assumed that Lord Hamilton, who had long served as Deputy Chairman, would take over, in fact, Hamilton also decided to resign at this moment. The Council were advised that they had the right to select their own Chairman and make new appointments to the Council; Lord Bute was thus succeeded in the chair by Lord Polwarth. This period also saw the inclusion among the Council's members of the heads of the Scottish art schools, *ex officio*, which formalised the arrangement whereby students, whose courses included measured drawing, augmented the collections. The Council were also active in acquiring new accessions and were frequently consulted in the development of the legislation that was to lead to the present system of protection for historic buildings. In these discussions Ian Lindsay took the leading part. Andrew Rollo, who had retired from Edinburgh City Architect's Department, carried out a number of pioneer researches among collections of historic drawings in the City's possession, as well as among those of the National Library of Scotland, including an important set of surveys by the Board of Ordnance depicting Scottish castles in the mid-eighteenth century. One of the last links with the war-time Record was broken when Stanislaw Tyrowicz, who had been appointed as the Record's draughtsman, emigrated to South Africa in 1952.

Haswell Miller's second important contribution to the Record came through his identification of a successor who could forge a pattern for its future development. While on a visit to Rome in 1951, Haswell Miller, who knew that he was about to retire and leave Scotland, met Colin McWilliam. McWilliam had just completed his architectural studies at Cambridge and had won a scholarship to Italy. This young English architect's artistic abilities were matched by his articulacy, and, after an interview in Edinburgh, which he had probably never visited previously, he rose rapidly through the ranks of the Record as draughtsman, and then Assistant Secretary, to emerge as Director after Miller retired in 1951. He joined the newly graduated Miss C H Cruft, who was already employed as a part-time researcher.

Miller's withdrawal provoked an accommodation crisis, because the Record could no longer hope to be sheltered under the Gallery's wing, and this led to a review of the Record's status. He wrote a letter describing his own hopes for the Record's future, which also reveals that its 'amateurishness' was inspired and carefully calculated. Miller was concerned that its strengths might not be fully understood by the parent body, the Ministry of Works, who had begun to investigate its activities, with a view to absorbing the young institution. In May 1953 he wrote to the Ministry:

'Before leaving I suggested to McWilliam he should draft a report on the situation as regards running and finance. This he has done very well and I am sending it to you herewith. (He has not included the "costs" part as the latest audit had not come through but I have suggested he shows you the summary of income and expenditure himself).'

'I was delighted and encouraged by the apparent good impression your Ministry's most unorthodox child seemed to make on Mr Wastie and Mr Keen when they attended the Meeting on 16 April. My team did their stuff admirably and have, I think, justified the confidence I had in them.'

'In regard to the new premises there is one point I had not considered. That is that whereas in the Portrait Gallery access could always be had to the Record material—the whole "family" there being acquainted with the set up—the Frederick Street place has to be shut up when both of the staff must be out. Clearly such an establishment must be available to the public and it is quite impossible to have it open at regular hours without a third body. Even a "Messenger" who could direct the enquirer to what he wanted. The more satisfactorily the present two do their recording the more they are liable to be out and in at irregular times.'

'Another point is the problem of safety. In the Portrait Gallery this was as complete as one could humanly expect. No smoking in the building, which is fireproofed and entirely under our control. Consequently we did not think about insurance. Now it seems essential to (a) insure what little is replaceable and (b) have photographic duplicates made of everything.'

Under Colin McWilliam's direction, the Record took on a new sense of purpose, which is clearly reflected in the Minutes. Although he prepared a number of measured drawings, he was perhaps too able an artist to relish the restricted expression of this medium, and he preferred to sketch directly on to the twin-lock index slips. Faced by unprecedented demolitions of country houses, he probably also realised that photography was vital if the handful of staff were to keep pace. Whereas, however, the earlier tradition of antiquarian recording had tended to favour the photography of isolated early architectural details, McWilliam brought a fresh eye to Scotland and an interest in decoration that was reflected in his unusually comprehensive surveys of country houses. Many of these were recorded during his researches on behalf of the newly-formed Historic Buildings Council from 1953; the recognition of the importance of the National Buildings Record's collections in the assessment of the architectural importance of structures eligible for grants brought a fresh impetus to their activities.

Colin McWilliam also initiated the photographic surveys of private collections that became so important a feature of the Record's development in Scotland. Although the Record had previously made photostats of historic drawings, the systematic photography of Scottish subjects in such collections as the Adam and Playfair Office Drawings in the Soane Museum in London not only stimulated the scholarship of Scottish architectural history, but gave a new string to the Record's bow, placing it on a par with art-historical photographic libraries in London like the Conway and the Witt collections.

These efforts and activities laid important foundations for the future. Dr David Walker, now Chief Inspector of Historic Buildings, but then a young student whose pioneering researches on Dundee architects had already brought him to the Record's attention, provides a vivid impression of its character in those early days:

'The Record was housed in a cool attic area lit by a long rooflight. Within I recall seeing Kitty Cruft perched on a very high, old-fashioned stool, working by the rooflight wall; she spent a good deal of time at a

typewriter with a very small typeface which seemed to have been especially bought for the oblong small-format topographical and architect files in green cloth boards (still in use today, although a great deal thicker now than they were then). On the other side were racks of the still familiar box-files of photographs, and screens, beyond which could be heard the off-stage noises of the Portrait Gallery staff. A few moments later I was handed over to Colin McWilliam, who had only recently arrived from Rome; I told him of my researches in Dundee, and we arranged to meet again. He and Kitty were then struggling with a flood of demolitions as a result of war-time requisitioning, building-licensing making repair difficult even for those who were disposed to retain their houses, as well as estate duty, then at record levels. As the Record was financed by a slender Treasury grant and the annual subvention had not allowed for inflation, still less the end of petrol rationing, no motor car could be provided. Colin and Kitty made their way as best they could by train, bus (taxis could not be afforded), and ultimately foot. As and when the College of Art allowed me the time, and my father could spare the car, I drove Colin to demolitions near Dundee, but I still well remember the long walk we made from the main Dundee–Arbroath Road to record Panmure and the offhand reception we received from the factor when we arrived there. Panmure was both an eerie and a thrilling place, still largely without electricity and quite unaltered since the 1850s having seldom been lived in following its

Panmure House, exterior, interior and detail of boss over stair; photographs by Colin McWilliam 1953

reconstruction by Bryce. Its three floors of state apartments, rather low-ceilinged for their massive plasterwork (some of it 17th-century and some of it by Bryce) and the huge scale-and-platt stair, the full height of the house, made a profound impression on me, the stair especially so as seen from the attic landing; the distance to the floor and the sheer scale of the central pendant, which one could almost reach out and touch, still linger vividly in my memory.'

Since there were more demolitions than Colin McWilliam and Kitty Cruft could cope with, David Walker was taken on as a fee-paid assistant for weekends and vacations. Dr Walker further recalls:

'By 1953 the Buildings Record was housed in a small but very pleasant suite of attic rooms over the architect A H Mottram's office in 14 Frederick Street, the main office being a sunny low-ceilinged room with a big bow dormer, its walls lined with files and drawings and its floors strewn with plans and box files. The fact that it was an absolute fire-trap did not occur to us. There, whenever college vacations allowed, I came through to see the collection of Burn drawings recently received from the RIBA, beginning my lifelong interest in the work of that architect; there were also the Charles Wilson drawings, the Adam drawings which Colin had recently photographed at the Soane, and the drawings which had been bought from the Bute Collection.'

'In 1954 the National Buildings Record was taken over by the Ministry of Works, and in the following year it was absorbed into the Ministry's headquarters at 122 George Street, a warren of old-fashioned business chambers formed by Peddie and Kinnear out of the Tontine Hotel. Its most memorable feature was the huge cantilever well stair with bunkers on the landings, since most rooms still had coal fires. The new room was austere and high-ceilinged, but somewhat dark since it looked out into a light well. The room, full of plan chests, soon became almost as cramped as Frederick Street had been, but somehow never achieved the same happy informal atmosphere.'

Eventually it became necessary to shed all part-time staff, who were not civil servants; Miss Cruft left in 1956, and in March 1957 Colin McWilliam resigned to take up a post at the National Trust for Scotland, which he had been helping on an informal basis. After Colin McWilliam's departure, the Record entered a brief fallow period, but in due time its organisation was regularised and in December 1958 the temporary post of officer in charge of the Record was advertised and Miss Cruft was appointed. However, despite leading a somewhat hand-to-mouth existence during its first quarter-century (in terms of official status and prospects), the Record had nevertheless built up the capacity to make itself a useful resource for a very wide range of researchers, as its correspondence files show. Professor Alistair Rowan, now Principal of Edinburgh College of Art, but in 1962 a young post-graduate, recalls his earliest experience of the record under Miss Cruft's charge:

'In the early 1960s the Scottish National Buildings Record was housed in cramped accommodation in a house on the south side of George Street. I first experienced the allure of its collections when as a raw post-graduate student I returned from Cambridge to Edinburgh to spend the summer of 1962 working on Robert Adam's romantic houses and the history of castle-style architecture in Scotland. I remember two things very clearly: the excitement of examining box after box of photographs of Scottish buildings, many labelled in the bold sloping hand of Colin McWilliam, recently the first director of the Record and a man whose knowledge of Scottish architecture was held in awe; and the fun of working with Kitty Cruft. Here was a person, prodigal in her expense of energy on behalf of others. I had been taught in Cambridge that a good research student should make full use of the services offered by the staff of any institution; I did not anticipate the generous foraging on my behalf by Miss Cruft, who seemed to have memorised the entire intricate structure of Scottish parish boundaries, who knew exactly where all the books were amid a guddle of shelves and plan chests, and who initiated a natty little index of the work of Scottish architects, bound into small green cloth files that had

the maddening habit of flapping shut the minute you consulted them!'

The Record's long spell under the roof of the Ministry of Works is reflected in a number of accessions to the collections. The most impressive is, unquestionably, the vast portfolio containing Col. Moody's 1859 scheme for additions to Edinburgh Castle, which he lugged to Windsor Castle, where he explained to a bemused Prince Albert that its perfect proportions were based on D R Hay's current researches into aesthetics.

During the mid-1960s there were moves to regularise the official standing of the Scottish National Buildings Record, which was recognised increasingly as a valuable national asset. These discussions were influenced by various factors, among them the current plans for the London Record. At the same time, more widely-based discussions were under way, both on the systematic recording of threatened buildings and on the creation of national archaeological archives to curate the growing body of field-survey and excavation records. Deliberations by a Treasury Standing Committee on Recording Ancient Monuments and Historic Buildings resulted in the recommendation that the National Buildings Record in London be incorporated into the English and Welsh Royal Commissions, and this was effected in 1963. Discussions in Scotland between the Ministry of Public Buildings and Works and the Scottish Royal Commission at this time concluded in the decision that the Scottish Record should also be transferred, as soon as suitable accommodation for the combined establishment could be found. The change in name to *The National Monuments Record of Scotland* resulted from the Treasury Committee's recommendation that all monuments—prehistoric and Roman remains and medieval earthworks—should be included; the material collected was to embrace records of excavations, where no other suitable repository existed.

Thus in 1966 responsibility for the Record passed to the Royal Commission on the Ancient and Historical Monuments of Scotland, and Commission and Record moved to enlarged accommodation designed as a base

The Library at 54 Melville Street (1966), formerly Sir Robert Lorimer's dining room

for the public archive of the latter institution and for the field-staff, drawing office and photographic departments of the former. The Commission's choice of a new home to house the conjoined bodies was a propitious omen for the future. The main building, 54 Melville Street, had been the town-house of Sir Robert Lorimer, and it still preserved much of its character, although Lorimer would have been astonished by the marquetry panel, symbolising the generation of electricity (complete with pylon), which had been installed in his rarefied, all-white drawing room and which was a souvenir of a previous tenant, the South of Scotland Electricity Board. The Record was established on the ground floor, with its main library in Sir Robert's dining room. This had been altered by him in what was a rather whimsical Gothic mode, for the Neo-Classical New Town, to accommodate a fine early tapestry. Although this was now displaced by shelves of books, much of the original detail remained, including

the fretwork ceiling with gilded bosses, the elongated stone chimney-piece dated '1904', with its enchanting tiles depicting tulips and birds, and the flimsy oriel window which intensified the heat in summer and imparted a chill during the winter, Although this was before the days when historic colour schemes became *de rigueur*, the original green and gold of the ceiling was carefully restored. This rich scheme had so depressed Lorimer's family that they dubbed the room 'the funeral parlour'.

The success of the amalgamation of the two bodies can also be symbolised by the reunification of the National Art Survey drawings. For in 1958, when the National Art Survey Publication Committee was finally wound up, considerable thought had been given to the disposal of the original drawings, whose execution had been initiated by Sir Rowand Anderson and whose ownership was then vested in the Trustees of the National Gallery. The collection included a duplicate set of tracings. In a compromise, it was decided that the Commission should receive the original drawings, while the Scottish National Buildings Record should receive the tracings. The justification for this was that the originals would be more carefully preserved by the Commission, whereas the copies were better suited to the intensive use that they would receive in the Record. Happily, in 1966 this collection of outstanding national importance was again brought together.

The Commission itself had by this time an extensive collection of plans, photographs, and a small library, which resulted from the preparation of county *Inventories*. The marriage of the Record to an institution which was primarily concerned with field-recording and publication was not without attendant problems, but with county-based box-files of photographs, the extension of the Commission's numbering system for negatives and plans, and the maintenance of the Record slip-index of buildings and architects, users steadily found their way around the amalgamated collection. Although much of the archaeological holdings had resulted from past *Inventory* surveys, the Commission collection also included material gathered in the course of the Emergency Survey of Marginal Land, undertaken between 1951 and 1958 in all parts

of Scotland where an expansion of agriculture or forestry was at that time expected.

Melville Street thus housed a fast-growing collection of archaeological and architectural material. The particular appropriateness of this location was heightened through the acquisition at this time of Sir Robert Lorimer's office drawings, the largest single collection in the Record's care. The rate of accession was reflected in the necessity to brace the adjoining 56 Melville Street with steel girders to carry the ever-multiplying plan-chests, while fire-detectors and security arrangements marked the collection's new status as an important national institution. The growth of the collections also made it possible to make a more than convincing case for extra staff, and Richard Emerson was the first of the Research Assistants who have helped to keep the Record a friendly and welcoming place for the young students who still comprise the largest single category of user.

The breadth of the collections also reflected the individual character of the Scottish Record, which made it an obvious model for the Irish Architectural Archive when that institution came into being. In London, the National Monuments Record specialised increasingly in photographs, because there were other institutions which collected architectural drawings and designs for the decorative arts. From its foundation in 1834, the Royal Institute of British Architects had sought to acquire designs by earlier generations of architects, while the Victoria and Albert Museum had made judicious purchases of designs from its foundation in 1852. In Scotland there had been no such safety-net to preserve design-drawings of national importance. Although the National Galleries have incidentally acquired a number of architectural drawings, their Prints and Drawings Collection has been directed towards the world of Fine Art, while the National Museums have never included a cabinet of design like their sister institution, the Victoria and Albert Museum in London.

Although there were several important collections of architectural drawings formed by Scottish architects, including Thomas Hamilton and John Lessels, these were dispersed in the salerooms. The Royal Scottish Academy's collection has as its core the diploma works of its members, and, while it contains many fine things, the number of drawings remains relatively small. The various attempts by Scotland's architects to found an Institute and associated local societies produced a small but important collection, but, on their successful federation by Sir Rowand Anderson in 1917, their energies were largely devoted to collecting portraits of earlier architects rather than their drawings. The preservation of the office drawings of the architect, William Henry Playfair, in the Library of Edinburgh University, following his death in 1857, was a unique accolade, reflecting his unusual status as part of the intelligentsia of the 'Modern Athens', while the office drawings of his professional brethren were all too often regarded as mere business papers and discarded. Happily, however, large numbers of drawings in the latter category have survived in family collections and institutional records—a typical result of the Scottish tenacity in preserving potentially useful legal and financial papers; this national attribute is reflected in the superb collections of both the Scottish Record Office and the associated local repositories, as well as the National Library of Scotland. Much of the energy of the National Monuments Record of Scotland has therefore been expended in making photographic surveys of private collections that not only illuminate the history of individual buildings, but also cumulatively help to present a more rounded picture of the biographies of individual architects.

The Record's incorporation in the larger body of the Commission ensured that it now had the benefit of a highly trained professional staff of photographers, draughtsmen and investigators, who brought their expertise to many of its established activities. Refinement of the legislation designed to protect historic buildings also required the Commission to record listed buildings prior to their demolition or alteration under the various Town and Country Planning Acts.

The archaeological collections were also increasing. This was due not only to a growing awareness of the importance of excavation archives, particularly for sites that had not been fully published, but also to the realisation that early illustrations of such monuments as stone circles and Pictish stones could make a valuable contribution to their present interpretation. Some collections of this kind were identified in the course of routine *Inventory* survey; for example, the series of glass slides built up by J Harrison Maxwell, which form an important link to the work of Ludovic Mann, resulted from research into excavations in Kintyre. The deposit by the Society of Antiquaries of Scotland of material relating to field-monuments and buildings gathered during the nineteenth and early twentieth centuries greatly widened the scope of the collections, the portfolios of drawings of brochs and stone circles prepared by Sir Henry Dryden in the later nineteenth century being among those most frequently consulted.

Changes in approach to the publication of archaeological excavations, which was the subject of discussion in the mid 1970s, stressed the importance of the proper curation of excavation archives as a vital adjunct to the dissemination of summary reports through journals and monographs. In consequence, the collections have been greatly increased by the working drawings, record negatives and slides for a variety of excavations in Scotland, and, as the depository for all excavations funded by Historic Buildings and Monuments (Scottish Development Department), the Record has a vital role in making this material accessible to students and researchers. Further enhancement was to come in 1983. The card-index and maps of the Archaeology Branch of the Ordnance Survey had formed an important source of information about sites all over Scotland since the establishment of the regional office in Edinburgh in 1958. The transfer to the Commission of staff and resources of the Ordnance Survey Archaeology Branch thus created a single archive of maps, cards, photographs and plans of all known ancient monuments in Scotland, handsomely achieving the goals espoused by those who had supported the ideal of a unified archaeological archive some twenty years before. Since 1976 the collections have been further augmented by the results of the annual programme of aerial photography undertaken by the Commission itself; this embraces both archaeological and architectural sorties, as well as those designed to record the changing industrial landscape. This photographic collection includes a high proportion of prints documenting totally new discoveries, whose recognition has led to a radically altered perception of the richness of our buried past.

The combination of the Buildings Record and the Royal Commission in 1966 thus laid the foundations of the most comprehensive assemblage of records relating to field monuments and historic buildings anywhere in the British Isles. Today it constitutes an unsurpassed and constantly updated source of information about *c*.100,000 sites and structures—a total that is still rapidly mounting. The initial pace of development of the conjoined Record was equally brisk, ensuring that the collection had already outgrown Melville Street by the early 1970s, and the plan-holdings had to be moved to a highly efficient, but unattractive, 'bunker' in the basement of nearby Meldrum House, in Drumsheugh Gardens. However, they were soon displaced again by the process of relocation among government offices that heralded the possibility of Scottish Devolution in 1976, and the drawings were then moved to 14 Atholl Crescent. The departure of the joint-tenant, the Ancient Monuments Branch, and the subsequent sale of these buildings, necessitated a further move. As a temporary solution, a short-term lease was accepted on 6–7 Coates Place, which had the principal advantage of being close to 54 Melville Street. If the Record was naturally sorry to exchange the sophisticated elegance of Lorimer's town-house for the rather bewildering suites of less carefully detailed rooms at Coates Place, the accommodation of the entire collection under a single roof was a boon for both users and staff. By 1990, however, the growth of the Record had ensured that part of the plan collection had to be sent back for storage in the strengthened structure of 56 Melville Street, and serious thought had already begun to be devoted to the necessity of housing the entire Commission in a single building.

The phenomenal growth of the collection has been the result of a number of factors. Those on the archaeological side have been briefly described above; those relating to buildings are, perhaps, more complex. For example, the high cost of office accommodation has made it difficult for architectural firms to retain large numbers of drawings (often incorporating material inherited from defunct practices), and the Record has frequently had to salvage large collections when the attics and basements in which they had slumbered were upgraded for other uses. Similarly, a number of institutions have decided to deposit their collections with the Record, where they enjoy enhanced protection as well as facilities for public access. In recent years, three collections of outstanding national importance have been deposited: the plans of Edinburgh's City Architect, the Property and Building Plans of George Heriot's Trust, and the drawings of the Northern Lighthouse Board.

An initiative that will doubtless prove important for the future has been the forging of close links with the Royal Incorporation of Architects in Scotland, whose historic drawings collection has also been deposited with the Record. The Incorporation's recent pioneering survey of architecture in Scotland dating to the 1930s alerted it to the necessity of making provision for the rescue of important collections of recent drawings, which all too often were being destroyed through lack of interest and appreciation. The Incorporation also realised that the expansion of their drawings collection could provide an important cultural resource, through exhibitions and publication, for the promotion and appreciation of Scottish architecture of all periods. These rapidly growing collections are deposited with the National Monuments Record of Scotland, and the two bodies have frequently acted jointly to save historically important collections on the brink of destruction. New attitudes to architectural collections in both Europe and North America have led to the recognition of the importance of preserving entire architectural archives, rather than merely the drawings, and also to the growth of Architectural Museums, whose representatives are now interlinked through the International Congress of Architectural Museums. These new ideas are reflected by the presence of models, medals, student drawings, sketches and office files among the joint-collections of the Royal Incorporation of Architects in Scotland and the National Monuments Record of Scotland.

This may seem a long way from the immediate war-time aims of 1941, but it is surprising how many of the Record's present activities can be traced back to the earliest days. Naturally, perhaps, many areas of the collections reflect the strong links with the founders, and it seems particularly satisfactory that figures like Ian Lindsay, who did so much to promote the preservation and appreciation of Scotland's architecture, are well represented. The historical collections, however, provide links with many earlier recording initiatives. The collections of David MacGibbon and Thomas Ross, the most celebrated of all Scotland's architectural historians, are interwoven with those of the Scottish National Buildings Record, the Royal Commission on the Ancient and Historical Monuments of Scotland (of which Ross was a Commissioner), and the Royal Incorporation of Architects in Scotland. The beautiful drawings of their predecessor in the recording of Scotland's architecture, R W Billings, can be found in the collection of the Royal Incorporation. The collections of the Society of Antiquaries of Scotland lead back even further, to the dawn of Scottish archaeology, through the work of James Skene, James Drummond, and Sir Henry Dryden.

If the modern survey material produced by the Commission dominates the accessions numerically, the necessity for the care of the historical collections has placed additional demands on the Record. The proposed new home of the Commission in purpose-adapted accommodation in Bernard Terrace will not only keep it in close contact with Edinburgh's other national research and recording institutions, but also provide the opportunity to improve the standards of care through enhanced environmental control. The necessity for a conservator has long been recognised, and indeed the post is essential, given the physical nature of the collections. The dominance of tracing paper in architectural offices from the late nineteenth century makes the preservation of collections like that of Sir Robert Lorimer especially labour-intensive. Ironically, perhaps, the poor quality of the war-time paper used by the Scottish National Buildings Record in its earliest days makes this another area requiring immediate attention.

The recognition of these challenges to Record staff comes at a time when Government has completed its own review of the work of the Royal Commissions. The Consultants who conducted the Review were favourably impressed with the Scottish Record; their recognition that it was under-resourced, especially in terms of staff, however, seemed to echo a familiar theme in its history, and the recommendation of a heightened profile won widespread approval. At the same time, new approaches to field-survey and publication underline the close relationship between the Record and the survey arm of the Commission, for the 'Inventory of Ancient and Historical Monuments and Constructions of Scotland', which the Commissioners were originally charged, by Royal Warrant, to compile, is now construed as the archive of the existing National Monuments Record of Scotland, where full details of all Commission survey programmes are publicly accessible. Publication, in a variety of formats will still be a vital Commission function, but future products in this field will represent, as never before, a distillation and selection of the information in the national archive. Computerisation will take the Record into an even further phase of development—a new era—opening up rich possibilities of retrieval, and increasing accessibility on a scale which matches the rapid growth and importance of the national collections.

Note

1 Stephen Croad, 'Architectural Records in the Archive of the Royal Commission on the Historical Monuments of England', *Transactions of the Ancient Monuments Society*, 33, (1989), 23–44.

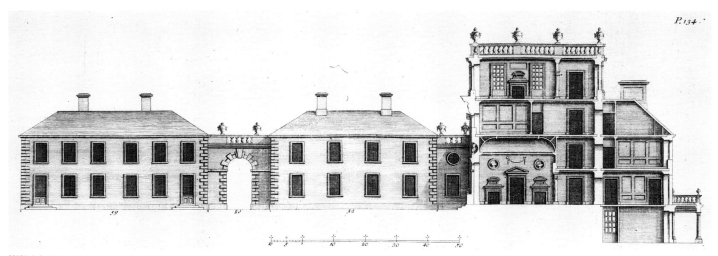

WILLIAM ADAM. *Rosehall House from*
'Vitruvius Scoticus'

ABBOTSFORD DRAWINGS

NMRS Photographic Survey of a collection of drawings for Abbotsford including: designs by John and Thomas Smith 1821; sketch designs by Edward Blore 1823; designs and working drawings by William Atkinson 1818–1823; designs for heraldic shields; elevations of principal rooms 1822; designs for furniture and carpets; sketches of interiors by M S Edmondes 1888; a bound volume of accounts (including Sanderson and Paterson, Builders 1816–1819; John and Thomas Smith 1820s; William Atkinson 1822; Edward Blore 1822; Nicholson and Hay 1824; William Trotter 1822; James Milne, Oil Gas Apparatus 1823–1824; William Baird, plasterwork 1824; William Henry Brown, stained glass 1823, etc.); a portfolio of designs for additions by William Burn 1853.
Copied 1985.

ABERDEEN ART GALLERY DRAWINGS

NMRS Photographic Survey of drawings in Aberdeen Art Gallery including: designs for Union Street Viaduct by James Young 1801, David Hamilton 1800 and John Rennie 1802; design for Victoria Bridge by Edward L J Blyth 1872; designs for Brucklay Castle by John Smith 1814; designs for Aberdeen Court House by John Smith 1814, and a house for Mr Carnegie by John Smith.
Copied 1969 (NMRS Inventory 20).

ABERDEEN, CLYDESDALE BANK DRAWINGS

NMRS Photographic Survey of plans in the possession of the Clydesdale Bank including: numerous designs for branches in the North East and North of Scotland; designs for the Town and County Bank, Aberdeen, by Archibald Simpson 1826; a design by an unidentified architect; a design probably by David Hamilton 1839; designs for the executed building by Archibald Simpson 1839; designs for subsequent alterations by James Matthews 1871 and William Kelly 1924, etc.
Copied 1969 (NMRS Inventory 17).

ABERDEEN PUBLIC LIBRARY DRAWINGS

NMRS Photographic Survey of drawings in Aberdeen Public Library including designs by John Smith for the Union United Free Church in the Shiprow, Aberdeen, and designs by Archibald Simpson for Mrs Emslie's Institution, 1837.
Copied 1967 (NMRS Inventory 19).

ABERDOUR CASTLE

Typescript of research files prepared by Dr M R Apted, while the author was an Inspector of Ancient Monuments (Scotland).
Presented by Dr Michael R Apted.

'ABERFELDY AND DISTRICT'

Two volumes of manuscript Insc.: 'Points and Places of Interest In and Around the Town of Aberfeldy being an Account, Descriptive, Historical and Geographical of Part of Central Perthshire. N Douglas Mackay, 1918.' Illustrated with photographs, sketches and survey plans of archaeological sites.
Deposited by Mrs S Yellowlees.

ABOYNE CASTLE

Sale Catalogue. 5th August, 1921 (Messrs Davidson and Garden, 12 Dee Street, Aberdeen). Illustrated.

WILLIAM ADAM (1689–1748), Architect

Vitruvius Scoticus; Being a Collection of Plans, Elevations, and Sections of Public Buildings, Noblemen's and Gentlemen's Houses in Scotland Principally from the Designs of the Late William Adam, Esq. Architect Edinburgh and London. No date, c.1811 *(Purchased by SNBR at sale of library of the Hon Sir Hew Hamilton-Dalrymple 1945 for £9.)*

Vitruvius Scoticus: a part collection of plates including several duplicates. Bound in with a set of pen and watercolour copies of plates from the Society of Dilettanti's *Antiquities of Ionia*, 1797. It is thought that this set of Vitruvius Scoticus plates may represent a

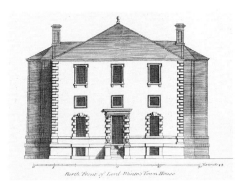

WILLIAM ADAM. Design for Minto House, Edinburgh, from 'Vitruvius Scoticus'

'rump' of Taylor's stock. Taylor was the London publisher of the volume.

Vitruvius Scoticus: A part collection of plates loosely bound.

ADAM DRAWINGS IN THE SOANE MUSEUM

NMRS Photographic Survey of designs by Robert and James Adam in the collection of Sir John Soane's Museum, London. All drawings thought to be for Scotland were photographed, as well as designs for patrons with Scottish surnames. Many designs remain unidentified. The collection was photographically surveyed by SNBR, in part, in 1953 and re-photographed in 1976.

WILLIAM ADAM TERCENTENARY EXHIBITION 1689–1989

Research files for the Exhibition held in 1989 at the Scottish National Portrait Gallery, Edinburgh, organised by James Simpson and the William Adam Trust.
Presented by the William Adam Trust, 1989.

THOMAS ADAMS

Album. Insc.: 'An Elegant Collection of interesting views in Scotland Representing Gentlemens Seats, etc.... With Descriptions Historical Descriptive and Traditional From the best Authors Interspersed with a Curious Natural History of Stones Dilligently compared and the best chosen' 'Thomas Adams 1812'. (The NMRS also holds an un-Grangerized copy of this book, *An Elegant Collection of Interesting Views ...*, 1802.)

NMRS collects these and purchases aerial photographs taken by other organisations or individuals. Aerial photographs in the collection include black and white and colour photographs taken by I A G Shepherd of sites and monuments in Grampian Region; Professor D W Harding in SE Scotland; G Harden in Highland Region; Dr S Driscoll, West Scotland; Professor G D B Jones, SW Scotland; and Dr W S Hanson, West Scotland.

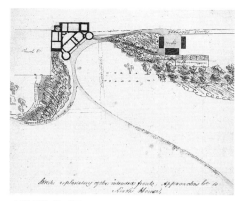

AIRTH CASTLE DRAWINGS. Design for approaches by D Hamilton 1806

AIRTH CASTLE DRAWINGS

A collection of drawings for Airth Castle and estate including: a garden design by William Boutchart 1721; late 18th-century plans for additions; designs for additions by William Stirling 1806 and David Hamilton 1806; and a design for planting apple trees in the walled garden 1829, etc.
Presented by Mr A F C Forrester, Airth Castle, 1971.

AERIAL PHOTOGRAPHS. Clatchard Craig, Fife, by Wing Commander G S M Insall c.1930

Important historic photographs from pioneering days of aerial photography in Scotland are also collected, including material by Wing-Commander G S M Insall, Flight Lieutenant E Bradley, and O G S Crawford, 1929-1941.

AERIAL PHOTOGRAPHS. Greenhillhead, Annandale and Eskdale, Dumfries and Galloway by RCAHMS

AERIAL PHOTOGRAPHS

The photographs from the RCAHMS annual aerial survey programme, begun in 1976, form a major and growing collection. In addition, the RCAHMS sponsors flying projects by individuals in different areas of Scotland. The

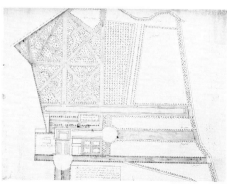

AIRTH CASTLE DRAWINGS. Landscape Plan by William Boutchart

GEORGE SHAW AITKEN. Competition entry for Glasgow City Chambers

GEORGE SHAW AITKEN (1836–1921), Architect

(RIAS) A small collection of exhibition drawings by George Shaw Aitken including a design for the Bank of Scotland, 34 and 34a Reform Street, Dundee, and a design for Amsterdam Exchange.

AMISFIELD HOUSE, East Lothian. Photograph taken during demolition

AMISFIELD HOUSE, East Lothian

(RIAS) Five photographs showing the house before and during demolition 1925, including an interior view of the dining room. The survey was organised by George Sinclair, Architect, Haddington, and presented to the EAA as a record.
(Filed with Henry Kerr Photographs).

SIR ROWAND ANDERSON (1834–1921), Architect

Xerox copy of Sir Rowand Anderson's Will, with extensive codicils relating to disposal of his property and collections, 1921.
Original with RIAS.

Xerox copy of a large Scrapbook compiled by Sir Rowand Anderson 1889–c.1910 concerning buildings designed by him; souvenirs of opening ceremonies; academic and professional distinctions; cuttings on the very wide range of subjects which concerned him, and letters to him from friends and colleagues.

SIR ROWAND ANDERSON. Portrait photograph

SIR ROWAND ANDERSON. 'Allermuir', his own house

The material was intended to be arranged by subject, but the system was never completed and the volume includes many loose cuttings
Original with RIAS.

(RIAS) Four photographs of 'Allermuir', Sir Rowand Anderson's own house, built to his design at Woodhall Road, Colinton,

SIR ROWAND ANDERSON. Dining room at 'Allermuir', his own house

Edinburgh c.1900, including: garden front, dining room and two views of the drawing room.
Presented by Robert Hurd and Partners.

SIR ROWAND ANDERSON DRAWINGS COLLECTION

NMRS Photographic Survey of designs now in the Special Collections Department of Edinburgh University Library, including a design for Haddo House by Wardrop and Reid c.1880; designs by Wardrop and Reid for Ballochmyle House 1880–1886; designs for Pollok House by Anderson, Simon and Crawford 1899–1904; and Mount Stuart, Bute by Sir Rowand Anderson 1876–1908.
Copied 1980   (NMRS Inventory 106).

WILLIAM ANDERSON, Builder, Edinburgh

A small collection of papers relating to the building contracts carried out by William Anderson (born 1872) including City and Guilds Certificate, notebook, schedules and plans.
Presented by his daughter, Dorothea Anderson 1984.

Anonymous. Edinburgh Castle from the Grassmarket

ANONYMOUS

Albums of cuttings and tracings showing churches and historic buildings c.1850 probably compiled by an architect (David Cousin?):

1 ('Scrapbook 1') Including: tracings of historic buildings illustrating different architectural styles through the ages and cuttings of churches and public buildings in Britain and Europe; Trinity College, Glenalmond; Pocket Chart of British Architecture by Archibald Barrington MD; the Scott Monument; traced and coloured sketches of historic buildings and castles in Scotland (Linlithgow, Holyrood, Old College, Glasgow); Design for West Church, Nicholson Street, Greenock, by David Cousin, pen and watercolour; a large collection of steel engraved letter-headings for Scottish Towns; and many designs for ornaments, including vases traced from James Gibb's *Book of Architecture*.

2 ('Scrapbook 2') An album devoted almost exclusively to cuttings relating to ancient and modern churches in Scotland, including many lithographed perspectives issued to subscribers, and an unidentified watercolour design for stained glass.

ANONYMOUS ALBUM OF ARCHITECTURAL DESIGNS c.1860–1870

A bound album of architectural designs and tracings for subjects mainly in the West of Scotland including: Arkleton House; Mr Robert Henderson's Villa, Belfast; Villa at Campsie; Parish School Dalziel; Theatre and Music Hall, Cowcaddens Street, Glasgow (Baylis' Theatre); Blantyre Parish Church;

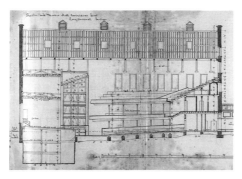

ANONYMOUS ALBUM OF ARCHITECTURAL DESIGNS. Section of Theatre in Cowcaddens Street, Glasgow

U P Church, Langbank; Barnhill Porter's Lodge; Monument at Ayr; Mission Church, Dobbie's Loan; U P Church, Ayr; Mr Robertson's Monument, Dunoon; Dolphinton Gate Lodge; Hamilton Burgh Buildings; design for a villa; Stanley villa, Pollokshiels; Mr Clark's villa, No. 3 Bourlie Hill; Mr Montgomerie's villa; Blantyre Farm for Mr MacPherson; Mr Thomas Reid's villa; Lodge at Haystoun House near Kirkintilloch; Lodge at Houston House dated 1865; J S Fleming's Tombstone at Campsie; Hunthill Stable Offices; Mr Turnbull's property, Jedburgh; Lady Belhaven's School, Wishaw; Theatre Royal, Glasgow, and Brisbane House Porch.

ANONYMOUS SKETCHES

A small collection of anonymous sketches of picturesque Scottish buildings including; Easter Coates House, Edinburgh; Kelly Castle (Angus); Red Castle; and Royston Castle (Granton), 1854.
Presented by Sir William Arbuckle, 1962.

Dr MICHAEL R APTED

Research files undertaken in connection with his Ph.D., *Painting in Scotland from the 14th to the 17th Centuries with Particular Reference to Painted Domestic Decoration 1550–1650*, University of Edinburgh, 1964. Includes files on individual buildings, photographs, extracts from documentary sources, etc. and a copy of the Ph.D. text and illustrations. (See also Aberdour Castle).
Presented by Dr M R Apted.

ARBROATH ALBUM

Photograph album with views of Arbroath by John Valentine c.1880.

ALEXANDER ARCHER. Col. Gardener's House at Prestonpans

ALEXANDER ARCHER (fl. 1830s), Artist

A large collection of pencil drawings by Alexander Archer depicting antiquarian subjects in Berwickshire, Edinburgh, Fife, Lanarkshire, Midlothian, Selkirkshire, Stirlingshire and West Lothian, 'drawn from nature' and dated 1834–1840, including prehistoric monuments, palaces, churches, castles, villages, mills and ancient trees.
(Purchased by SNBR from Mrs McQueen Ferguson for £30, 1950.)

ARCHITECTS' INVENTORIES AND TESTAMENTS

An index with dates and page references to the inventories and testaments of Scottish architects, craftsmen and some allied trades in the Scottish Record Office, extracted by Ierne Grant and relating to Edinburgh and Glasgow.

ARCHITECTURAL MODEL OF AN UNIDENTIFIED INSTITUTION

Painted wood design model of a small institutional building of cruciform shape and with a belfry bearing an anchor on a tablet over the principal door. Possibly a seamens' mission hall. Scottish, c.1860.

ARDGOWAN HOUSE DRAWINGS

NMRS Photographic Survey of plans for Ardgowan including: design for Ardgowan by Wardrop and Reid 1882; designs for alterations to Ardgowan by William Burn 1862; design for the staircase to tea garden by R S Lorimer 1905; design for a railing by Ramsay Traquair 1912, etc.
Copied 1984 (NMRS Inventory 157).

ARDKINGLAS DRAWINGS. Design for a 'Marine Pavilion' by James Playfair

ARDKINGLAS DRAWINGS

NMRS Photographic Survey including designs for Ardkinglas by unidentified late 18th-century architect, James Playfair 1790, A M Binning 1832, and William Burn 1831.
Copied 1967 (NMRS Inventory 1).

Part collection of designs for Ardkinglas including: an unidentified late 18th-century design for a new classical house with bow; perspective view of proposed new house by James Playfair 1790 (title page from his portfolio); and a miniature set of proposals by William Burn 1831 including a perspective view and annotated floor plans.

ARDMIDDLE HOUSE, Aberdeenshire

Notes on the Stained Windows Etc. in the Hall Ardmiddle House Aberdeenshire, 1873. Printed by G Cornwall and Sons, Lithographers, Aberdeen. With descriptions of windows by Clayton and Bell, London, and the Frieze (after engravings published at London in 1842 of drawings by James Byres of Tonley 1760–80, depicting sepulchral caverns of Etruria) apparently also executed by Clayton and Bell. Description of marbles including Statue of Torquato Tasso, by Torelli of Florence, purchased at International Exhibition, London, 1872; bas reliefs by Miller; the Drawing Room ceiling after especially commissioned casts by George A Lawson, London; and brackets of Hiawatha and Minnehaha by Miss Mary L White, Aberdour, 1867.

PHOTOGRAPHS OF ANCIENT TOMBS IN ARGYLLSHIRE

Photograph album, Insc.: 'Photographs of Ancient Tombs in Argyle-shire', containing a photographic survey of the carved grave-slabs and ancient monuments of Argyllshire, including Kilmartin, Castle Sween, etc. and including views of villages, etc. Possibly produced as a limited edition, c.1870s.

R B ARMSTRONG, Antiquarian

A collection of sketches, rubbings and lithographs prepared by R B Armstrong and mainly concerning medieval buildings in the South-west of Scotland including a series of sketches taken from an early manuscript illustration of Castle Milk preserved at Hatfield House.
Society of Antiquaries of Scotland, Manuscripts.

AUCHENTORLIE HOUSE. Elevation of entrance front by D Hamilton 1813

AUCHENTORLIE HOUSE

A small collection of designs for castellated additions by David Hamilton 1812–1813 and Robert Lugar 1815.

AUCHMACOY HOUSE DRAWINGS

NMRS Photographic Survey of drawings at Auchmacoy House including a watercolour of the house 1789, and plans for farm buildings by W Christie 1870.
Copied 1969 (NMRS Inventory 22).

AULDBAR CASTLE DRAWINGS. Roos' design for the drawing room ceiling, with splashes of distemper received during execution

AULDBAR CASTLE DRAWINGS

A collection of designs for Auldbar Castle and Estate including a few c.1820 for additions attributed to John Paterson; the majority by Alexander Roos 1843–44 for the castle and gardens, including a highly finished design for Pompeian painted decorations for the drawing room ceiling; a design for a pentagonal porte cochère attributed to R W Billings and several designs for lodges, stables and farm buildings by unidentified designers.

AYR: KYLE AND CARRICK DISTRICT COUNCIL DRAWINGS

NMRS Photographic Survey of drawings in the collection of Kyle and Carrick District Council Architect's Department including: designs for Ayr Assembly Rooms by Thomas Hamilton 1827; alternative designs for Ayr Town Hall, 1878; design for Ayr Town Hall by James Kennedy Hunter 1901; designs for alterations to Ayr Town Hall by J and J A Carrick 1937; drawings for St John Baptist Tower by James Kennedy Hunter 1913–1915; survey of Craigie House by James Kennedy Hunter 1921; designs for Wallace Tower, Ayr, by Thomas Hamilton c.1830 and additions 1886; designs for Rozelle House, Ayr, by William Burn 1825 and David Bryce 1829–1830; designs for proposed alterations to Rozelle by Allan Stevenson and Cassels 1930–1932, etc.
Copied 1977   (NMRS Inventory 81).

AYR PUBLIC LIBRARY PHOTOGRAPHS

NMRS Photographic Survey of historic photographs of Ayr and vicinity in Ayr Public Library.
Copied 1976   (NMRS Inventory 66).

AYR TOWN HALL

Estimates for reconstruction of Ayr Town Hall, J Kennedy Hunter, Architect, Ayr, 1901.
Deposited by Carnegie Library, Ayr.

BALBIRNIE DRAWINGS

NMRS Photographic Survey of drawings for Balbirnie House including: designs for Balbirnie House by Richard Crichton 1815, Thomas Leadbetter 1896–1897, Bertram and Son, London 1896, James Gillespie 1912, and Guy Elwes 1947; designs for lodges by David

Bryce 1860 and 1874; designs for Newtonhall House attributed to David Bryce 1829; and many designs for estate buildings, gasworks, etc. (Drawings now in SRO).
Copied 1974   (NMRS Inventory 57).

BALLINDEAN HOUSE. Perspective view

BALLINDEAN HOUSE

Portfolio. Design for additions. Perspective view, plans and sections c.1830. (Design attributed to the owner William Trotter, but in office style of Thomas Hamilton)
Deposited by Walter Campbell, 1971.

BALMACAAN ALBUM

Photograph album, Insc.: 'Balmacaan, these photographs all taken with my little Kodak. Cornelia Craven' c.1910, including exterior and interior views.

BALMORAL ALBUMS

NMRS Inventory of photographs of Scotland in the collection of Her Majesty the Queen at Balmoral and Windsor Castle.
Listed 1979   (NMRS Inventory 92).

BARHOLM HOUSE DRAWINGS. Working drawing by Robert Adam

BARHOLM HOUSE DRAWINGS

A small collection of drawings for Barholm House including designs by Robert Adam 1789; the associated working drawings; and designs for stables and estate buildings by unidentified architects.

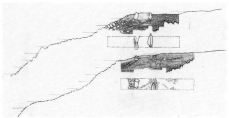

PROFESSOR GERHARD BERSU. Drawn sections of Bersu's excavation at Traprain Law, East Lothian

PROFESSOR GERHARD BERSU (1889–1964)

Negatives, drawings, notebooks and correspondence of the excavations at Scotstarvit Covert homestead 1946–7; Green Craig homestead 1946–7; and Traprain Law fort 1947. There had been a preliminary visit to Scotland in 1939, but it was not until after the Second World War that Bersu was invited to excavate these sites; the collection amply demonstrates his skills and techniques, in particular the use of colour on site drawings, already used at various sites in England, including Little Woodbury, Wiltshire, and the Isle of Man.
Presented by the Department of Environment, 1973.

URSULA V G BETTS (née BOWER) (1914–1988)

Famous for her anthropological research on the Nagas in India, Mrs U V G Betts resided from 1952–1967 on Mull, where she became interested in the local archaeology. The collection in NMRS comprises colour slides, correspondence, notes and excavation

drawings of surveys and minor excavations of various sites on Mull.
Presented by U V G Betts.

ERSKINE BEVERIDGE. Excavation photograph; Bac Mhic Connain, Vallay, North Uist

ERSKINE BEVERIDGE (1851–1920)

A collection of glass negatives and photographs of archaeological sites in the Western Isles and pencil drawings of pottery from North Uist. Beveridge was an enthusiastic antiquarian and photographer who travelled extensively, visiting, surveying or excavating sites, and publishing his results with J G Callander in the *Proceedings of the Society of Antiquaries of Scotland* in 1931 and 1932 and in his own volumes on *Coll and Tiree*, 1903 and *North Uist*, 1911.

BIEL DRAWINGS

NMRS Photographic Survey of drawings for Biel House including: designs for additions to Biel by William Atkinson 1806–1809; designs for Biel Chapel by Wardrop and Anderson 1886; designs for alterations by Robert Lorimer 1920; and many designs for estate buildings.
Copied 1980   (NMRS Inventory 151).

BIEL HOUSE DRAWINGS

A collection of designs for Biel House including designs attributed to John Paterson for a new house c.1800.

BIEL HOUSE DRAWINGS. Design for S front

Presented by Mr A M Dalgleish of Mottram, Patrick, Dalgleish, as part of their office drawings 1984.

THE BIRMINGHAM GUILD LTD

Illustrated Brochure of metalwork. No date, c.1930. Includes some work in Scotland.

ALEXANDER BLACK (1798–1858), Architect.

Engraved portrait after William Bonnar RSA, published 1851.
Prov.: Heriot's Hospital Trust.

BLACKBARONY ALBUM

Photograph album with a survey of Blackbarony House, interior and gardens, 1926.

BLAIR CASTLE DRAWINGS

NMRS Photographic Survey of Blair Castle drawings including: designs for kennels at Dunkeld by Robert Dickson 1853–1855; design for offices at Dunkeld by James Winter 1744; plans for New Town of Dunkeld by Robert Reid 1806; designs for a school and teacher's house at Dunkeld by Robert Dickson 1855; designs for alterations to Blair Castle by J Macintyre Henry 1903; designs for alterations to Blair by R and R Dickson 1840–1841; designs for Dunkeld Palace by Thomas Hopper 1820s; designs for Dunkeld House by R Macintyre Henry 1898; designs for Dunkeld

Church by Archibald Elliot (after 1814); competition drawings for Logierait Poorhouse; designs for garden buildings by Roger Morris; design for a bridge by Abraham Swan; designs for gardens mid-18th century; designs for Chinese railings by Richardson; designs for Blair Village by R and R Dickson; designs for stucco-work at Blair Castle 1740s; designs for alterations at Blair Castle by George Steuart late-18th century; designs for additions to Blair Castle by John Douglas 1748 and James Winter 1743; and many designs for shooting lodges, estate buildings and gardens.
Copied 1971   (NMRS Inventory 53).

BLAIR CASTLE MUNIMENTS

Typescript abstract of payments for craftsmen, architects, etc., during the 18th century.

BLAIRQUHAN DRAWINGS

A collection of working drawings for Blairquhan House by William Burn 1824.
Deposited on indefinite loan by Sir James Hunter Blair, Bt.

BO'NESS IRON CO. LTD

Catalogue. Drainage, lampposts, brackets, gutters, etc, 1928. Dock Foundry, Bo'ness. Illustrated and priced.

Catalogue. Selection of Gates & Panels for Houses, 1937. Dock Foundry, Bo'ness. Illustrated.

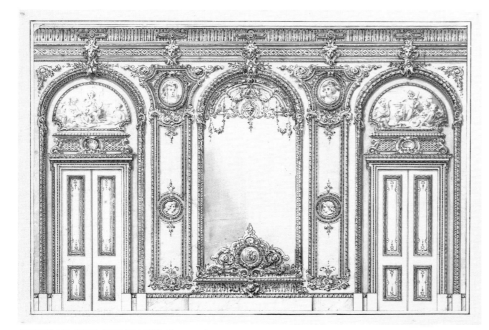

BONNAR AND COMPANY. Decorative scheme exhibited at the 1862 Exhibition

BONNAR AND COMPANY (c.1845–c.1960), Interior Decorators.

A large collection of designs by this firm, founded c.1845 by Thomas Bonnar I in partnership with Robert Carfrae. The designs include a record drawing of the staircase ceiling at Penicuik House painted in 1782 by the house-painter Thomas Bonnar, father of Thomas Bonnar I; design for Queen Victoria's Waiting Room at Paddington Station; design for the firm's contribution to the 1862 Exhibition including: Lothian Road U F Church, Edinburgh; Falkland Palace 1895; and St Bernard's Well, Edinburgh, etc.; surveys of early Scottish painted decorations including: Mary of Guise's House, Edinburgh; Earlshall; Pinkie; and many modern designs in the same idiom c.1845–1950.
Presented to the Scottish National Buildings Record by Mrs Bonnar, 1958.

THOMAS BONNAR II

Album of decorative details and source material including: photographs of early Scottish painted decoration (some from drawings by the firm); continental mural decoration; details from medieval illuminations; designs for unidentified ceilings, and a panel for Milton House School, Canongate, Edinburgh; a printed bookcover c.1750; a Christmas card from Mr and Mrs Bonnar, and a photograph of his drawing room at 7 Ann Street, Edinburgh, c.1880–1900.

BONSHAW TOWER

Research notes and correspondence relating to Bonshaw Tower compiled by A M T Maxwell-Irving.

BOUCHER AND COUSLAND. Design for a double villa for T L Paterson

BOUCHER AND COUSLAND, Architects

Album. Bound volume, Insc.: 'Villas Designed and Executed by Boucher and Cousland Architects Glasgow', containing highly finished record elevations and plans of villas in suburbs of Glasgow and Clydeside and described by style, 'Italian', 'Gothic', 'Old Scotch', 'Elizabethan', 'Rustic' and 'Swiss'. Some of these villas still exist e.g. 4 Sydenham Road and 4 and 6 Albert Road. One of the elevations has an '1858' date panel. The volume was presumably compiled to assist potential clients select a house design. The house owners are identified, e.g. 'Erected for James Morton Esq', and an inexpensive double villa in the Swiss style is credited as being erected for the architects themselves.

M BOUQUET. View of North Berwick

M BOUQUET, Artist (1819–1876)

A collection of views of Scotland including: North Berwick Harbour; Tantallon Castle; Urquhart Castle; Linlithgow Palace; and Invergarry Castle.

BOWHILL HOUSE, BUCCLEUCH DRAWINGS

NMRS Photographic Survey of drawings for Bowhill including: designs for Bowhill by William Atkinson 1812 and William Burn 1831–1833; monument to Sir Walter Scott by Rickman and Hussey 1835; landscape designs for Bowhill by Thomas Gilpin; designs for additions to Royston House (Caroline Park, Edinburgh) attributed to William Adam 1740; lithographed plans for the Edinburgh Winter Gardens by Pilkington and Bell 1875; plans of a model showing proposed additions to Dalkeith House 1831 by William Burn; designs for additions to Collegiate Church of St Nicholas, Dalkeith, by David Bryce 1847; designs for Irvine House (?) by Henry Holland 1783; drawings of Montagu House, Whitehall by Anthony Salvin 1829; design for Montagu Bridge, Dalkeith, by William Chambers after 1770; survey of Brunstane Estate by John Slezer 1690s; designs for alterations to Dalkeith House by James Craig 1775–1776; designs for a Gateway to Dalkeith Palace by William Tait 1794, James Adam 1794, John Robertson and James Playfair 1786; and a volume of plans of the Buccleuch Estates by William Crawford and Sons 1810.
Copied 1976   (NMRS Inventory 49).

BRADFORD UNIVERSITY SCHOOL OF ARCHAEOLOGICAL SCIENCES

Notebooks, drawings, photographs and negatives, and colour slides of archaeological surveys of sites in the Orkney Islands: Fara, 1982; Cava, Rysa Little and Switha, 1983.
Presented by J R Hunter and S J Dockrill.

CHARLES BRAND, Demolition Contractor, Dundee

File of press-cuttings relating to buildings demolished by this firm with press advertisements for subsequent sale of materials from Panmure, etc., 1949–1958 and a typescript list of buildings demolished.

A collection of pencil drawings illustrating buildings demolished by this firm (posthumous portraits from photographs, etc). Drawn by Colin Gibson.
Deposited by Dundee Museums and Art Galleries.

CHARLES BRAND, Demolition Contractor, Dundee. The demolition of Murthly (New) Castle

Two albums of photographs of country houses and castles demolished by Brand from 1945, including many dramatic press photographs showing blasting, etc. Includes Logan, Murthly (New Castle), Panmure, etc.
Deposited on temporary loan by Dundee Museums and Art Galleries, 1987.

BROGDEN DRAWINGS

NMRS Photographic Survey of a collection of early-18th-century designs belonging to Dr W Brogden, including a plan for the garden at Saltoun Hall by Henry Fletcher of Saltoun and plans of the gardens at Spottiswoode.
Copied 1972   (NMRS Inventory 38).

ALEXANDER BROWN (BROWN AND WATT), Architect

Xerox of an album of press-cuttings and memorabilia compiled by Alexander Brown, Architect, relating to buildings designed by him in Aberdeen and district 1873–1917, with additional press-cuttings relating to later family history.
Copied per Miss Brown.

DAVID BRYCE. Carte-de-visite portrait

DAVID BRYCE (1803–1876), Architect

A set of exhibition perspectives showing buildings designed by David Bryce and Office including Ballikinrain, Blair, Craigends, Cullen, Drum Castle, Fyvie and Langton. (Almost all exhibited at RSA. A portrait of Bryce, in chalk, which accompanied the drawings, was passed on to the Scottish National Portrait Gallery).
Presented to SNBR by the Law Department of the Bank of Scotland 1942.

(RIAS) Two exhibition drawings of designs for the Albert Memorial Keep, Edinburgh Castle, 1864, and the Library for the Royal College of Physicians, 9 Queen Street, Edinburgh, 1876, being the sole survivors of a large collection of Bryce material left to the RIAS and dispersed during the 1930s.

(RIAS) Carte-de-visite portrait photograph, full length by G & D Hay, Photographers, 68 Princes Street, Edinburgh.

Microfilms of Albums containing tracings and sketches of 'Scotch and Old English Ornament' and 'Ornamental Sculpture' compiled by David Bryce. (Originals in Bryce Collection, George Washington University, St Louis, Missouri, USA).

Examples of Ornamental Sculpture. Photocopy of a volume of tracings, mainly from French 18th-century sources, in the Bryce Collection of George Washington University, St Louis, Missouri, USA.

Plaster bust after George MacCallum *Presented by James Morrison, Perth.*

DAVID BRYCE. *Blair Castle, perspective view and The Royal College of Physicians, Edinburgh, design for a new library*

THE BUILDING CHRONICLE. *Lithograph of the National Gallery of Scotland*

THE BUILDING CHRONICLE

The Building Chronicle, Vol. 1, Nos. 1–41, May 10th 1854–August 1857. Published by John Greig and Son, Melbourne Place, Edinburgh.
   This rare, profusely illustrated monthly journal, modelled on *The Builder*, gives a

particularly vivid insight into Scottish architecture and the building trades.

BUILDINGS OF THE SCOTTISH COUNTRYSIDE

Research data collected by the project fieldworkers during this survey of 23,000 rural buildings conducted by Robert J Naismith, of Sir Frank Mears and Partners, who were commissioned by the Countryside Commission for Scotland. Includes: record sheets, computer data; questionnaires; negatives, photographs and contact sheets; correspondence 1978–1981, etc. The conclusions were published in Robert J Naismith, *Buildings in the Scottish Countryside*, 1985.
Deposited by the Countryside Commission for Scotland, 1985.

CAPTAIN W ST G BURKE, Royal Engineers

Portfolio of sketches, plans and notes made by W St G Burke whilst employed on the Ordnance Survey of Orkney and Shetland in 1875 and presented to the Society of Antiquaries of Scotland in 1886.
Society of Antiquaries of Scotland MSS 165.

GEORGE BURN (fl. 1800–1813), Builder

Portfolio. Alternative designs for a small house, one with two stories and Gothic wings attached by quadrants and a cheaper single storied version. S.: 'George Burn'. No date.

WILLIAM BURN (1789–1870), Architect

The office set of working drawings (the sketch designs, perspectives, are in the British Architectural Library Drawings Collection). A very large collection of working drawings for palaces, public buildings, monuments and country houses throughout Scotland, including: Edinburgh Academy; North Leith Church, Edinburgh; St Giles' Cathedral, Edinburgh; St Mary's Episcopal Church, Dalkeith; Camperdown House; Garscube House; Whittinghame; Dupplin Castle; Tyninghame House; Milton Lockhart; Bowhill; Gosford

CAPTAIN W ST G BURKE. Drawing of Maes Howe, Orkney

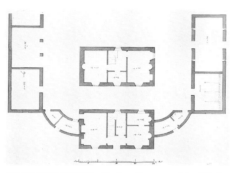

GEORGE BURN. Design for an unidentified house

House; Castle Menzies; Hamilton Palace, etc. *Presented by Miss Browne, 1952, and per Royal Institute of British Architects, 1953.*

BUTE

see RENFREWSHIRE AND BUTE

BUTE DRAWINGS

NMRS Photographic Survey of drawings for Bute estates including: designs for Dumfries House by R Weir Schultz 1894–1905; the South front of Culzean Castle by D Wilson

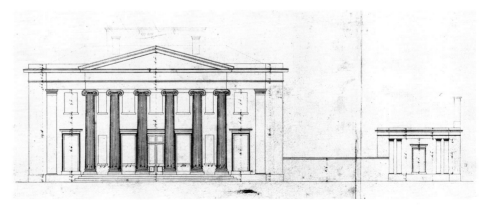

WILLIAM BURN. Design for Camperdown House

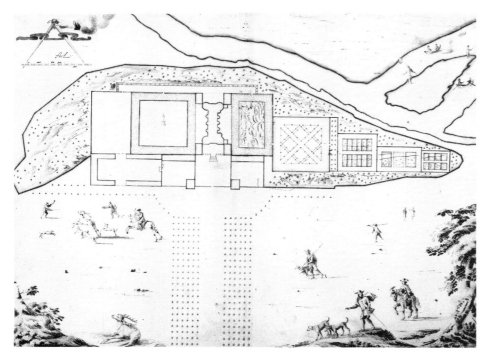

BUTE SALE DRAWINGS. Thirlestane Castle: design for landscape attributed to John Slezer

1793; survey of Mochrum Castle by Richard Park 1873; designs for Dumfries House by the Adam brothers 1754; design for the Earl of Dumfries's Gallery in Cumnock Church 1755; contract for building Dumfries house 1754; etc.
Copied 1984 (NMRS Inventory 160).

BUTE SALE DRAWINGS

A collection of drawings from the Bute Collection, including: plans of Thirlestane Castle and grounds attributed to John Slezer 1670s; a design for Melville House c.1700; a design for an unidentified house c.1700; and designs, attributed to Roger Morris, for Whitton Park for the Earl of Islay c.1740.
Purchased 1952 by SNBR from Horace G Cousin, Bournemouth.

'THE CAIRNS', CAMBUSLANG.
Photograph Album; view of drawing room

'THE CAIRNS', CAMBUSLANG

Photograph Album, Insc.: 'The Cairns 1858' and 'To Mrs John P Kidston with Mr Burnet's Compts. Sept. 1875'. The album was probably first bound up to contain a set of photographic copies by T Annan of the architect John Burnet's designs for J P Kidston's Baronial villa, 'The Cairns' at Cambuslang. The survey photographs of the exterior and interiors were probably taken and added immediately prior to the album's presentation.

CALLENDAR HOUSE, FALKIRK

Sale Catalogue (Contents), Tuesday 8th October 1963. Dowell's Ltd. On the premises.

CALLENDAR HOUSE DRAWINGS

NMRS Photographic Survey of Callendar House Drawings including designs by James Craig 1785; David Hamilton 1827; designs for additions by Wardrop and Reid 1869–1876; designs for estate buildings and farms; and a design for St Andrew's Parish Church, Edinburgh, late 18th-century.
Copied 1971 (NMRS Inventory 37).

CALLY HOUSE AND ESTATE DRAWINGS

NMRS Photographic Survey of drawings in Cally Estate Office of plans for additions to Cally House by Lanyon and Lynn c.1857 (not executed).
Copied 1978 (NMRS Inventory 85).

CAMBRIDGE UNIVERSITY COLLECTION OF AERIAL PHOTOGRAPHS

Collection of aerial photographs of sites and monuments in Scotland taken by CUCAP, from 1945 onwards; selected for acquisition on a regular basis.
Purchased from CUCAP.

CHARLES CAMERON DRAWINGS

NMRS Inventory and photographs of the Charles Cameron drawings in the Department of Drawings, Hermitage Museum, Leningrad.
Listed 1961   (NMRS Inventory 79).

CAMMO HOUSE

Inventory of furnishings at Cammo House, 1897.
Presented by Vanessa Emerson.

CANAAN LODGE, EDINBURGH. Album

CANAAN LODGE, EDINBURGH

Photograph album with a survey of the exterior and interiors of Canaan Lodge, Morningside, Edinburgh, after completion of additions by the architect, James B Dunn, 1907.

CANISBAY CHURCH

Report by Hippolyte Blanc, Architect, 1891.
Provenance unknown.

CARDY HOUSE COLLECTION

NMRS Photographic Survey of plans and photographs at Cardy House, Lower Largo, Fife, including: plans for property and cottages in Lower Largo (including 'Crusoe Property'

1864–1935 by Gillespie and Scott and James Gillies, etc.); plans for additions to Freuchie Mills; and a collection of photographs including an album with views of Edinburgh by Nacara and Co.
Copied 1978   (NMRS Inventory 96).

DAVID CARR (1905–1988), Architect

Designs for Kirkcaldy Town Hall 1937–1956.
Deposited by Stewart Tod, 1982.

ALEXANDER CARRICK (1883–1966), Sculptor

Two volumes of copy letter books of outgoing correspondence of Alexander Carrick (Vol I: 1920–1931, Vol II: 1931–42) concerning sculpture commissions, including many War Memorials.
Presented by Mrs Scott, daughter of Alexander Carrick, 1973.

J AND J A CARRICK, Architects

(RIAS) A collection of drawings by J and J A Carrick including: designs for Ayr Ice Rink 1937; Coatbridge Public Baths 1935; Kirkcaldy Municipal Buildings; Rothesay Municipal Pavilion; Stair House 1934; House at Ottoline Drive, Troon 1937–1938; and a large collection of photographs.

CARRON COMPANY

Architects' Catalogue: Grates, Fire-irons, Cooking Apparatus, Ranges. No date, *c*.1910. Fully illustrated.

Catalogue of Register grates, interiors, dog grates, hob grates, mantel grates, fire dogs, fire backs, casings, fenders and fire irons. January 1911. Carron Works. Illustrated.

CARRONHALL

Photograph album including a survey of exterior and interior of Carronhall, May 1916; loose mounted photographic surveys of

CARRONHALL. Album; view of entrance front

Glenbervie House and Gardens and Carbrook House, Grounds and Lodges.
Presented by Scottish Record Office, ex Carron Company Records.

W LAIDLAW CARRUTHERS, Architect

The office drawings including designs for: Strathmashie Lodge *c*.1895; Invertrossachs 1912; The Parsonage, Altyre; St Mary's RC Rectory, Huntly Street, Inverness, 1888; Cluny Castle; Eilean Aigas House 1905; Kinrara 1904; Tannery Buildings, Inverness 1900; Dallas Lodge 1901; Dunbar's Hospital, Inverness 1900; Moy Hall 1895; Belladrum 1895; Altyre House 1900.
Presented by Alexander Grant, Inverness.

CARSE HOUSE

Specification, Insc.: 'Specification and description of the work of a house to be built at Carse in the Valley of Coulnaulen in the Parish of Kilberry Argyllshire', 1828.

CARTE-DE-VISITE ALBUM

Photograph album of an anonymous collector Insc.: 'Photos collected on my journeys' *c*.1860, with a wide selection of photographs of castles, towns, churches and bridges throughout Scotland, including a view of White Horse Close, Edinburgh, by Archibald Burns.

CARTE-DE-VISITE ALBUM. St Ronan's Well, Innerleithen

CASSILLIS ESTATE OFFICE DRAWINGS

NMRS Photographic Survey of drawings in Cassillis Estate Office, including designs for cottages and estate buildings 1879–1907.
Copied 1979 (NMRS Inventory 93).

CASTLE FORBES DRAWINGS

NMRS Photographic Survey of drawings at Castle Forbes including: a portfolio of designs for Castle Forbes (Putachie Castle) by John Paterson 1807; designs for a New House at Putachie by John Paterson 1811; designs for Castle Forbes by Archibald Simpson 1813–1815; designs for a castellated lodge by John Smith *c*.1834; a design for the policies mid-18th century; and designs for estate buildings. (These drawings are now in SRO).
Copied 1974 (NMRS Inventory 54).

CASTLE STUART PLANS

NMRS Photographic Survey of designs by Brown and Wardrop 1869.
Copied 1968 (NMRS Inventory 15).

CAWDOR CASTLE ALBUM

Photograph album with views by J Valentine of exterior and interiors of Cawdor Castle *c*.1890, and views of Helmingham Hall and Peckforton Castle, including many interiors.

PROFESSOR V GORDON CHILDE. Photograph of Childe at Skara Brae, Orkney

PROFESSOR V GORDON CHILDE (1892–1957)

Collection of negatives of archaeological sites and monuments in Scotland including Childe's major excavations at Skara Brae neolithic settlement 1927–30; Finavon fort 1933–35; Castle Law fort, Glencorse 1931–32; and Berries Burn fort 1939. Childe was Abercromby Professor of Prehistoric Archaeology at Edinburgh University 1927–46.
Presented by RCHME and Institute of Archaeology, University of London.

Within the collection are two notebooks and a large number of negatives, illustrating monuments in Argyll, Perthshire, and Angus, dating from Childe's appointment as a Commissioner 1942–43. Childe's original excavation notebooks have been deposited in the Institute of Archaeology, University of London; copies of the Scottish material are held in the NMRS.

ALEXANDER CHRISTIE, Artist

Manuscript history of the Edinburgh School of Design from 1760, extracted from the Minutes of the Board of Manufacturers *c*.1855.

GEORGE AND FREDERICK CHRYSTAL PHOTOGRAPHIC COLLECTION

A large collection of photographic negatives taken by George Chrystal (Professor of Mathematics at Edinburgh University) and his son, Frederick, principally of Edinburgh subjects and dating from 1900–1930. A set of their prints was presented to Edinburgh City Library.
Presented by the Chrystal family.

CLAPPERTON STUDIOS, Selkirk, Photographers

NMRS Photographic Survey printed from negatives, taken by Clapperton Studios, of architectural subjects in the Border region, including views of many country houses, (e.g. Bowhill *c*.1930), towns and villages.
Printed 1968–1970.

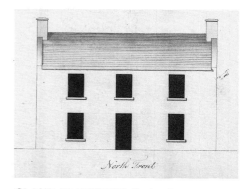

CLAUD CLEGHORN. Design for an unidentified house

CLAUD CLEGHORN (fl. 1800), Builder

Portfolio. Design for a Farmhouse 'Edin(burgh) 1 June 1796'. S.: 'Geo. Robinson and Claud Cleghorn'. Plans and Elevations.

CLERK OF PENICUIK DRAWINGS

NMRS Photographic Survey of the Clerk collection including designs (many by the family themselves) for the following properties: Elie House; Drumlanrig Cascade; designs by John Plaw for a lodge; designs for Penicuik House by John Baxter; designs for Mavisbank House; design for a library by James Clerk; designs for the stables at Penicuik House; design for St Mungo's Church, Penicuik by James Clerk; plan of Kinross House and grounds attributed to Alexander Edwards; and an engraving of a design for Marchmont House by Thomas Gibson.
Copied 1968 (NMRS Inventory 3).

NMRS Photographic Survey of a portfolio containing surveys of the Clerk estates by John Ainslie 1796.
Copied 1986 (NMRS Inventory 158).

CLERKINGTON ESTATE, East Lothian

Sale Catalogue. Auction by Messrs Bernard Thorpe and Partners, 1951. Photographically illustrated, showing House and Farm buildings, etc.

H E CLIFFORD (1852–1932), Architect

A collection of designs by H E Clifford including: House at Troon for Frederick N Henderson 1905; House at Milngavie for Michael Diak 1922; Cathcart Manse 1902–1903; Golf Club House at Elliot for Arbroath Golf Club (no date); Shennanton for W Loudon McNeil 1908–1909; Torrisdale Castle 1904–1908; Perth City Hall 1908; St Germain's, Bearsden 1903–1904; Cour, Kintyre 1919; Highlanders Memorial Church 1921; Scotstoun UF Church 1905; Whitecraigs 1898; More's Hotel 1921; Sorn Church 1910; Titwood Established Church 1894; and a large collection of student drawings by James Bunyan 1921–1925.
(NMRS Inventory 162).

Specifications for renovation of Imperial Hotel, Buchanan Street, Glasgow 1918; proposed Picture House, East Miller Street, Denniston 1920; and slater-work, for the Distillers Co. Ltd, Port Dundas (Frank Burnet & Boston Architects). Folder of cuttings from catalogues concerning chimney-pieces.

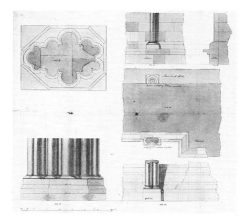

COLDINGHAM PRIORY DRAWINGS.
Details of piers

COLDINGHAM PRIORY DRAWINGS

A collection of designs and record drawings executed in connection with the restoration of Coldingham Priory by the architect, William J Gray, of Gray and Paterson, 1835–1858. Includes designs for new work in the style of the original and surveys of old work removed during restoration.
Deposited by the Berwickshire Naturalist Club, 1979 (NMRS Inventory 95).

FREDERICK R COLES

Ordnance Survey 1 inch:1 mile map annotated by F R Coles showing the areas of Aberdeenshire and Kincardineshire surveyed in 1899. As Assistant Keeper of the National Museum of Scotland, Coles was employed by the Society of Antiquaries of Scotland to survey the stone circles of NE Scotland, publishing his results in the *Proceedings* of the Society 1899–1905.
Presented by A MacLaren.

DR JOHN X W P CORCORAN (1927–1975)

Collection of photographs and drawings from research and excavations, mainly of chambered cairns in Wigtownshire and Caithness, 1961–72, reflecting the contribution to megalithic research made by Corcoran, while he was a lecturer in the Department of Archaeology, University of Glasgow.
Presented by SDD.

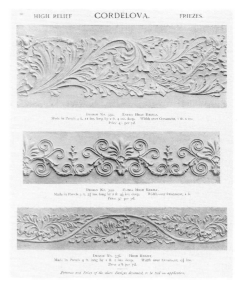

THE CORDELOVA COMPANY LTD.
Catalogue

THE CORDELOVA COMPANY LTD

Cordelova. The Embossed Decoration for Walls, Ceilings, Friezes, Dados. Catalogue and Price List.
No date, c.1900.
The Company's Works and Head Office were at 45 Pitt Street, Edinburgh.
Purchased 1981.

JOHN M CORRIE (1882–1938)

An Investigator with the Royal Commission

1925–1938; the J M Corrie notebooks are held in the RCAHMS collection.

Also held are copies of other notebooks containing sketches and notes on artefacts, customs and the history of SW Scotland, as well as poems by J M Corrie and his father, J Corrie.

COWDENKNOWES DRAWINGS

NMRS Inventory of drawings for Cowdenknowes House and Estate.
Listed 1978   (NMRS Inventory 76).

INNES OF COWIE ALBUM. View of the terrace at Ellon Castle

INNES OF COWIE ALBUM

Photograph album with a collection of art photographs and photographs of Cowie House and neighbouring properties, including Ellon Castle, Raemoir, St Andrews, etc. *c.*1860.
Presented by Christie's, South Kensington, 1988.

F & S COX LTD

Catalogues of *Electrical Supplies*, including *Electric Bells, Telephones, Electric Light Accessories, Electrical Fixtures* 1904 Head Office: 83–87 Farringdon Road, London. Fully illustrated.

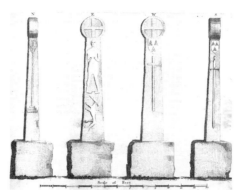

ARCHIBALD CRAIG SCRAPBOOKS

ARCHIBALD CRAIG SCRAPBOOKS

Albums (three volumes), Scrapbooks compiled *c.*1825–50 by Archibald Craig (38 Fountainhall Road, Edinburgh). The Craigs ran a cloth warehouse on the South Bridge, and the albums, which reflect Archibald's diverse interests, include engravings and sketches of buildings in Edinburgh and vicinity, and an unidentified architect's design for a Monument to General Sir Ralph Abercromby (*d.*1801).

CRAIGIEHALL DRAWINGS

NMRS Photographic Survey of drawings for Craigiehall including: designs for additions by Thomas Brown 1818; designs by William Burn 1828; designs by David Bryce 1852; design for stained glass at Craigiehall by Messrs Ballantine; survey of Blackwood House, Lesmahagow *c.*1829; late 17th-century design for a house; designs by Sir William Bruce; design for garden layout by William Boucher; designs for Craigiehall Temple attributed to John Adam *c.*1755; and many designs for estate buildings.
Copied 1983   (NMRS Inventory 149).

CRAIGSTON CASTLE DRAWINGS

NMRS Photographic Survey of drawings at Craigston Castle including: 18th-century designs for an unidentified house and Craigston Castle; sections of rooms at Craigston 1751; designs for alterations and additions by John Smith early 19th century and a scheme by 'Mr William Adams of the fields about the house of Craigstoun 1733'; bound volume with plans of Cromarty Castle 1746–1747 and 18th-century designs for Craigston Castle; bound volume with plans of farms on Craigston Estate 1780 and 1782; bound volume of plans of estate 1770–1779; plans and designs for gardens by James May 1749 and Charles W Crosser *c.*1875; design for a greenhouse attributed to John Smith; and a plan of the West Indian estates.
Copied 1967 and 1982   (NMRS Inventory 11).

JAMES HEWAT CRAW (1880–1933)

Collection of photographs, notebooks and correspondence reflecting Craw's wide and varied interests in archaeology and natural history. Of particular interest are photographs of his excavations at Broch of Gurness 1929–33 and Dunadd fort 1929–30, as well as contemporary archaeologists including Professor V G Childe, J G Callander and W Grant. The correspondence reflects the extensive research undertaken by Craw for his publications.

Other material by Craw is included in the RCAHMS collection. Survey drawings of monuments in Berwickshire by Craw were used by the Royal Commission for the revised *Inventory* in 1915.

Craw was employed by the MoW to undertake the excavations of the Broch of Gurness 1929–33, and his excavation drawings are held in the NMRS.
Presented by SDD.

CRAWFORD PRIORY DRAWINGS

NMRS Photographic Survey of drawings at Crawford Priory including: estimate for additions by Alexander Raes, Mason in Ceres; designs for Crawford Lodge attributed to James Craig c.1780; survey and designs for additions to Cults Parish Church 1873; design for Pitlessie Mill 1869; and designs for estate buildings.
Copied 1970   (NMRS Inventory 25).

JAMES E CREE. Portrait photograph

JAMES E CREE (1864–1929)

Three notebooks by J E Cree relating to the excavation of caves at Inchnadamph 1926, undertaken with J G Callander and J Ritchie. A rancher in America for many years, Cree returned to Scotland and became an active archaeologist, his major excavations including Traprain Law fort, with A O Curle, 1914–23.
Society of Antiquaries of Scotland MSS 632.

CRIMONMOGATE DRAWINGS

NMRS Photographic Survey of drawings at Crimonmogate House including designs by Archibald Simpson c.1825, and designs for subsequent alterations.
Copied 1969   (NMRS Inventory 18).

CROMARTIE DRAWINGS

NMRS Photographic Survey of drawings in the Cromartie Collections including: designs for Tarbat House by J McLeran, late 18th century; plans for alterations at Castle Leod c.1912; and designs for estate buildings.
Copied 1980   (NMRS Inventory 138).

A R CROSS

File of research notes and condition reports relating to the *Survey of Late Medieval Sculptured Stones in Argyll* from 1950, and draft of interim report. (The report was initiated by the Ancient Monuments Board, of which A R Cross was a member.)

J BRIAN CROSSLAND. New Register House, Edinburgh

J BRIAN CROSSLAND

A collection of finished drawings used as illustrations for J Brian Crossland's many articles on Scottish architecture and scenery, including a few from his *Victorian Edinburgh*, 1966. With a set of scrapbooks of the series including 'Journey of the Clyde' *Glasgow*

J BRIAN CROSSLAND. Physicians' Hall, Edinburgh

Herald, 1967; 'Writer's Landscapes' *Glasgow Herald*, 1968; *The Weekly Scotsman* 1959–1965, and *The Scotsman* 1959–1962. The collection includes a research file compiled by J Brian Crossland on Frederick Thomas Pilkington, the Scottish Victorian architect, between 1957 and 1961.
Presented by Mrs Audrey Crossland, 1989.

CULLEN HOUSE DRAWINGS

NMRS Photographic Survey of drawings for Cullen House including: designs for additions to Cullen by David Bryce 1858–1861; designs for proposed additions to Castle Grant by Andrew Kerr 1883; designs for Balmacaan House c.1818; designs for shooting lodges and estate buildings; landscape designs by T White 1789, and estate plans by Peter May of Cullen and Findlater 1762 and 1764; designs by James Playfair including design for a new castle at Cullen 1789; designs for additions at Cullen 1789; design for Cullen Town Hall 1788; design for a burying-ground at Cullen 1789; design for a Temple in the flower garden 1788; design for the Temple of Pomona 1788; and a plan for altering the Bridge 1788. (These drawings are now in SRO).
Copied 1969   (NMRS Inventory 24).

CULLODEN HOUSE. Sale catalogue; the President's Room showing Bonnie Prince Charlie's Bed

CULLEN HOUSE

Sale Catalogue of contents. September 22 1975 Christie, Manson & Woods.

CULLODEN HOUSE

Sale Catalogue of contents 21st July 1897, A Fraser and Co., Inverness. Photographically illustrated with survey of principal rooms, Bonnie Prince Charlie's Bed, etc.
Purchased 1984.

CULZEAN CASTLE DRAWINGS

A large collection of drawings for Culzean Castle including: designs for a villa for Sir T Kennedy by James Adam 1755; designs for Culzean Castle by Robert Adam 1777–1779 and 1787 with related designs for chimney-

CULZEAN CASTLE DRAWINGS. Design for a villa for Sir Thomas Kennedy

pieces, glasses, etc; design for a ruined bridge by Robert Adam 1787; and many designs for estate buildings by James Gillespie Graham 1815 and Robert Lugar, etc.
Deposited by The National Trust for Scotland 1990. NMRS Photographic Survey 1973 (NMRS Inventory 52).

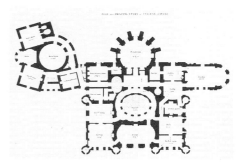

CULZEAN CASTLE DRAWINGS. Ground-floor plan of Culzean Castle

ALEXANDER O CURLE (1866–1955)

A O Curle was the first Secretary of the Royal Commission 1908–1913, and the material in the RCAHMS collection comprises his field notebooks, personal diaries and an illustrated excavation report of Jarlshof 1932. The personal diaries offer a remarkable insight into the work and experiences of A O Curle from 1908, when he started the work of the Commission with an entry '1st Aug 1908. The private journal of a wandering Antiquary', through his experiences during both World Wars, until the final entry in 1954.

CECIL L CURLE (1901–1987)

A collection of photographs and negatives of incised and sculptured stones in Scotland, and excavation photographs of the Brough of Birsay settlement 1936–7. Married to A T Curle, son of A O Curle, Mrs Curle was particularly interested in Early Christian stones, publishing several papers in the *Proceedings of the Society of Antiquaries of Scotland* and *Antiquity*.
Presented by C L Curle.

JAMES CURLE (1862–1944)

Copies of notebooks with sketches of the pioneering excavations at Newstead Roman fort 1905–1909, by J Curle (brother of A O Curle).

CECIL L CURLE. Mrs Curle examining cross-slab No. 2, Meigle, Perthshire

G RONALD CURTIS

Research notes, index cards and survey material relating to Military Roads and Bridges in Scotland.

RANDALL POOLE DALE

Album. Copy of Samuel Leith (Lithographer), *The Tradesmans Book of Ornamental Designs.* No date *c*.1847. Insc. on Cover: 'ORNAMENTAL DESIGNS BY RANDALL POOLE DALE 1847', interleaved with four original pen drawings (which are probably the finished drawings for the plates) and a design for a cabinet in pencil.

DALMENY CHURCH MASONS' MARKS

Research files and survey sketches prepared by A J Turner while studying the incidence of masons' marks in Dalmeny Church, 1950s.

RANDALL POOLE DALE. Design for wallpaper

DALQUHARRAN CASTLE DRAWINGS

NMRS Photographic Survey of drawings for Dalquharran Castle including: two letters from Robert Adam to Thomas Kennedy 1786 and 1789; an Inventory of 1837; a survey of the estate by Hugh Rodger 1781; designs for additions by Wardrop and Reid 1880; Letting Particulars for 1893, 1903 and 1904; and a photograph album showing the Castle and Estate c.1885.
Copied 1980   (NMRS Inventory 111).

DARLEY HAY PARTNERSHIP, Architects

NMRS Survey of Plans in the Darley Hay Partnership, Architects, Ayr 1880–1963. Inventory arranged alphabetically by location.
Listed 1977   (NMRS Inventory 87).

MISS HILDA MAY DARLING'S COUNTRY HOUSE ALBUM

Postcard album, compiled by Miss Hilda May Darling, with views of Scottish country houses collected 1902–c.1930.

DARNAWAY CASTLE MUNIMENTS

NMRS Survey of Moray papers at Darnaway including: abstract of accounts for Donibristle House and Chapel by Alexander McGill and carving by Robert Henderson; abstract of building accounts for Darnaway Castle by Alexander Laing 1802–1809; abstract of papers relating to Moray Place, Edinburgh by William Burn 1822 and James Gillespie Graham 1823.
(NMRS Inventory 13).

W R DAVIDSON (d.1945), Architect

A collection of exhibition drawings of his designs for villas in Nairn and the North of Scotland, by W R Davidson, 8 New Square, Lincoln's Inn, London, c.1912.

R DAWSON SKETCHES

A collection of sketches of Picturesque Scottish subjects and the Lake District

W R DAVIDSON. Design for an unidentified house

1833–1839. Including: Abbotsford; the Canongate, Edinburgh; Loch Lomond; Melrose; Portstewart; Stirling Castle; and the Trossachs Inn.

DESERTED MEDIEVAL VILLAGES

Research files, index cards, air photographs, etc., relating to their investigation 1968–1975.

JOHN DEWAR COLLECTION

A collection of colour and black-and-white photographs and negatives of sites and

JOHN DEWAR COLLECTION. Aerial photograph of Jarlshof, Shetland

monuments throughout Scotland, mainly scheduled and guardianship sites, commissioned by Historic Buildings and Monuments, Scottish Development Department, 1965–74.

DISCOVERY AND EXCAVATION IN SCOTLAND (DES)

Correspondence and the original entries sent to the Council for Scottish Archaeology (CSA) (formerly CBA Scotland), for inclusion in their annual publication, have been deposited annually since 1977 by the editors.
Presented by DES per E V W Proudfoot.

PHILIP W DIXON

Typescript study 'Fortified Houses of the Border Area' (Public access only with author's permission).

DOBIE AND SON LTD, Interior Decorators

NMRS Survey of documents, photographs and designs in the possession of Dobie and Son, founded 1849, including: ledger and estimate books 1857–1860; album of press-cuttings 1868–1959; printed list of commissions for ecclesiastical work 1859–1929; photographs of premises 1900–1975, etc.
Copied 1981.

DOLLAR ACADEMY DRAWINGS

A collection of designs for Dollar Academy by William Henry Playfair 1818–1821; designs for alterations 1887; and site plan for a house by Playford Reynolds.
Deposited by the Governors of Dollar Academy Trust, 1971.

M E M DONALDSON (1876–1958) NEGATIVE COLLECTION

NMRS Photographic Survey of the collection of negatives taken by M E M Donaldson (and now in Inverness Museum) of subjects principally in Argyll and Invernesshire,

including castles, archaeological and historical sites, cottages, monumental sculpture and towns.
Copied 1981   (NMRS Inventory 127).

JOHN DOUGLAS. Design for Traquair House

JOHN DOUGLAS (fl.1730 to c.1778), Architect

The office drawings, including: a set of student drawings copied from Gibb's *Book of Architecture*; a survey of 'Bonnyton'; designs for Arniston, 'Archerfield', Newton House, 'Wedderburn', Roseneath, Finlayston, Traquair, Lochmaben Tolbooth and several unidentified subjects; a copy of the side elevation of Inveraray after Roger Morris and a series of house designs on playing cards. The collection also includes a survey of 'Trinity or Bowlie Bay in the Island of Jersey' by 'Robert Douglas 11th May 1779' and a set of watercolour diagrams to accompany lectures on surveying methods.
Presented by the Company of Merchants of the City of Edinburgh, 1985, as part of the Rev. John Sime Collection.

Contract dated 17th June 1747 between William Nisbet of Dirleton and John Douglas, Architect in Edinburgh, for building an addition to Archerfield.
Presented by Mottram, Patrick, Dalgleish as part of their Drawings Collection 1981.

John Douglas's copy of James Gibbs, 'A Book of Architecture', second edition 1739, bearing an inscription 'Mr James Adams Brother to John Adams Architect in Edinr. Borrowed from Mr Douglas Inigo Jones' works for which his receipt lies in my hand not being returned JD. Ja: Adams receipt for this book lodged

with Earl of Dalhousie to whom I have given the book JD', and bearing the Earl of Dalhousie's Bookplate. (The Earl of Dalhousie was both a patron and executor of John Douglas's estate.)
Purchased with a 50% grant from the Friends of the National Libraries, 1989.

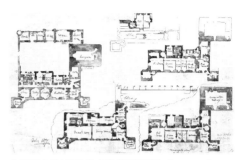

DRUM CASTLE DRAWINGS. Survey plans 1877

DRUM CASTLE DRAWINGS

A collection of drawings from Drum Castle including: a design for the walled garden c.1800; an antiquarian survey of the old tower 1876; a survey of the house c.1870; a proposal by David Bryce to build a Baronial screen across the entrance court 1876; a design for additions 1877 by John Bryce; working drawings for additions by John Bryce 1878–1880; and a plan for a bathroom by John Bryce 1893.
Presented by W Schomberg Scott, 1979.

DRUMLANRIG, BUCCLEUCH DRAWINGS

NMRS Photographic Survey of the Drumlanrig Drawings including: drawings by Clerk of Eldin depicting Dumfries and Drumlanrig estate; designs for Montagu Bridge, Dalkeith by Robert Adam 1791; designs and working drawings for alterations at Drumlanrig 1864–75; design for a Bridge over the River Nith at Dumfries by Thomas Boyd 1792; designs for a chapel at Drumlanrig by George Gilbert Scott; designs for Morton Church by William Burn 1839; and designs for a very

large number of estate buildings, including Thornhill.
Copied 1978 (NMRS Inventory 49).

A DRUMMOND

Albums. Two volumes of press-cuttings, engravings and a few original drawings relating to archaeological and antiquarian subjects and mainly relating to Edinburgh apparently compiled by 'A Drummond, Craiglea Drive, Edinburgh' 1905–1944.

THE REV. A L DRUMMOND

A collection of papers relating to his researches on Scottish Presbyterian Churches, including negatives, photographs, plans, guidebooks and some correspondence 1930s. *Presented by Mrs Christine McWilliam, 1989, as part of the McWilliam Collection.*

JAMES DRUMMOND. View of Elphinstone Tower

JAMES DRUMMOND (1816–1877), Artist

Album. A volume of antiquarian sketches and finished drawings of castles, tower houses, town houses and market crosses, etc., throughout Scotland 1840–1861. Many of the drawings of market crosses are dated 1861 and were drawn in connection with Drummond's research for his paper to the Society of Antiquaries of Scotland in that year.
Society of Antiquaries of Scotland MSS 386 (NMRS Inventory 99).

Two portfolios of sketches Insc.: 'Sculptured Monuments of Iona and the West Highlands', with sketches of monumental sculpture on Iona and including: Seton, East Lothian; Kilmichael; Strachur; Kilmartin; Poltalloch; Kiels; Kilmory; Killean; Kilkerran; Kilkivan; Saddell; Kilavon; Balquhidder; Ettleton, Roxburghshire; and Dunbar 1860–1875. After Drummond's death the collection was published by the Society of Antiquaries of Scotland as *Sculptured Monuments of Iona and the West Highlands*, 1881.
Society of Antiquaries of Scotland MSS 166 (NMRS Inventory 101).

Sketchbook of archaeological and antiquarian subjects including the Cat Stane; a sketch of a gargoyle from the Cowgate (at Lixmount Villa?); a sketch of a pair of spurs; Musselburgh Market Cross; a jointed stool in Biggar Kirk dated 1694; a recumbent tomb at Carnwath; Covington Castle; a carved stone built into a wall at Liberton Tower; sketches at Traquair House and the Bear Gates; thatched cottages 1860–1863.
Society of Antiquaries MSS 44.

An album of tracings from J Stuart's *Sculptured Stones of Scotland* said to have been copied by James Drummond. From the collection of Professor G Baldwin Brown. *Deposited by the Department of Fine Art, University of Edinburgh per Dr Higgett.*

SIR H E L DRYDEN. The North Gate, Wisby, Gotland

SIR H E L DRYDEN (1818–1899)

An archaeologist and antiquary, and much acclaimed for the accuracy of his plans, Dryden travelled extensively in England, France and Scotland, surveying numerous upstanding monuments. He spent several seasons 1851–91 in Orkney, Shetland and West Scotland, where he worked closely with George Petrie and surveyed many monuments, including brochs such as Lingro (now destroyed). This collection comprises hand-drawn copies of the sketches, plans, and annotated drawings, many in colour, executed by W Galloway. The original drawings are in the Central Library, Northampton, near Dryden's home at Canons Ashby.
Society of Antiquaries of Scotland MSS 21–24, 27, 30, 223, 493.

(RIAS) Wooden box containing the results of a visit to Visby, Gotland in 1876 including; manuscript notes; translations; portfolios of plans, elevations and details of churches of Visby; watercolours of the Town Wall and St Hans Gatan; and an exhibition catalogue of The Viking Club, London, 1906, referring to part of this collection.

Three portfolios of surveys of churches in Orkney and Shetland, and surveys of chapels including: chapel on the Brough, Deerness; Wyre; Eynhallow; Chapel at Linton, Shapinsay; Egilsey; Kirk of Ness, Yell; chapel at Westray; St Ola's Chapel, Bridge Street Lane, Kirkwall; Old Church, Orphir; chapel on the Brough of Birsay; chapel at Culbinsbrough, Bressay; Uyea Chapel; St John's Church, Norwick; Kirkaby, Westing, Unst; Meal Colvindale, Unst; St Margaret's Chapel, Edinburgh Castle; chapel on the North shore of head of Holland; Halcro Chapel, South Ronaldsay; St Tredwell's Chapel, Papa Westray; chapel at Swandro, near Westness, Rousay; Chapel of St Mary, Lybster, Reay, Caithness; and chapel on Inchkenneth, Mull.
Society of Antiquaries of Scotland MSS 25, 26 and 190 (NMRS Inventory 102).

DUFF HOUSE DRAWINGS

A collection of designs for Duff House by David Bryce, Junior, 1870.

DUNBAR DEAN OF GUILD DRAWINGS

NMRS Survey of Drawings in Dean of Guild Collection, Dunbar 1893–1919.
Listed 1978   (NMRS Inventory 86).

DUNBEATH CASTLE ALBUM

Photograph album with views of Dunbeath Castle, Thurso and vicinity *c.1890.*

DUNDEE ALBUM

Photograph album with views of Dundee *c.1875,* mainly by J Valentine, but with a few amateur photographs.

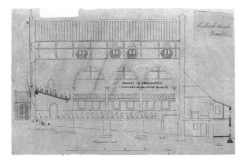

DUNDEE DUPLICATE PLANS. Cross-section of design for Rosebank Church

DUNDEE DUPLICATE PLANS

A large collection of designs for buildings in Dundee submitted for approval by the Dean of Guild including designs by most of the leading architects and builders in Dundee *c.1867–1883* and several architects outside Dundee (including G F Bodley, David Cousin and Pilkington and Bell, etc.) Inventory arranged by architect.
Deposited 1968 by Town Clerk, Dundee   (NMRS Inventory 83).

DUNMORE PARK. Design for the entrance front by William Wilkins

DUNDUFF HOUSE ALBUM

Photograph album with a survey of Dunduff House (Perthshire) and gardens *c.1890.*

DUNIMARLE DRAWINGS

NMRS Photographic Survey of drawings for Dunimarle Castle including working drawings by R and R Dickson 1837–1845.
Copied 1971   (NMRS Inventory 30).

DUNMORE PARK

Portfolio. Design for a new house. Plans and elevations (William Wilkins *c.1820).*

DUNN AND FINDLAY, Architects, Edinburgh

The Office Drawings (also incorporating many of the office drawings of Mottram, Patrick, Dalgleish, who had inherited the collection). A very large collection including the following designs by Dunn and Findlay: Bellevue Hotel, Dunbar 1895; 'The Scotsman' Offices, South Bridge, Edinburgh 1899–1902; a survey of Bonnington House, 1914; alterations to Blair Drummond 1921; alterations to Jenner's, Princes Street and J & R Allan's, South Bridge, Edinburgh 1920s; Jenner's Depository,

DUNN AND FINDLAY. F T Pilkington's design for John Ballantyne's house at Walkerburn

Balgreen Road, Edinburgh; and George Watson's College, Edinburgh, 1929; also many designs for smaller houses in Edinburgh and East Lothian, and including 'The Bield', Elgin 1928. A H Mottram's drawings include: designs for Hampstead Garden Suburb; designs for H Avray Tipping in Wales; designs for Rosyth from 1916; and many housing projects throughout Scotland. (This collection included a number of historic drawings, among them the designs for Biel and the contract for Archerfield by John Douglas, (listed separately) and tracings of David Bryce's designs for The Glen, etc.).
Presented by Mottram, Patrick, Dalgleish, 1981.

DUNPHAIL DRAWINGS

NMRS Photographic Survey of drawings for Dunphail including: designs for Edenkillie Manse attributed to John Paterson 1814; portfolio of designs for Dunphail by John Paterson 1820; a working drawing for Dunphail by W H Playfair 1827; and designs for Kinnaird House, Stirlingshire (including a late 18th-century plan showing the furniture arrangement on the second floor).
Copied 1985 (NMRS Inventory 161).

DUNPHAIL HOUSE DRAWINGS

NMRS Photographic Survey of Dunphail House Drawings including: design by John Baxter 1787; portfolio of designs by John Paterson c.1819; designs by W H Playfair 1827–1828; design for proposed additions by Alexander Ross 1878–1879.
Copied 1978 (NMRS Inventory 89).

DUNROBIN CASTLE DRAWINGS

NMRS Photographic Survey of drawings for Dunrobin Castle including; plans attributed to Alexander McGill 1720, John Adam 1776 and James McLeran c.1785 and a portfolio of designs for additions by Charles Barry, drawn by Peter Keir 1845.
Copied c.1965 (NMRS Inventory 120).

DUNROBIN PHOTOGRAPH ALBUM

Photograph album, Insc.: 'Scotland' and bearing cipher of the Duke of Sutherland, including views of Dunrobin Castle and Sutherland estates c.1900.

DUNS CASTLE DRAWINGS

NMRS Photographic Survey of drawings at Duns Castle including: designs by John Baxter 1792 and 1794; Richard Crichton 1817; designs and working drawings by James Gillespie Graham; design for additions by Bonomi and Corry, Durham 1847; designs for a Tolbooth and for Christ Church, Duns.
Copied 1972 and 1988 (NMRS Inventory 43).

DUNURE HARBOUR

NMRS Survey of documents relating to Dunure Harbour including: accounts for expenditure on New Harbour 1810–1814; Act of Parliament 6th May 1811; and printed proposals for improvement 1897.
Copied 1980 (NMRS Inventory 111).

DUNVEGAN CASTLE ALBUM

Photograph album with a survey of Dunvegan Castle, interiors and estate c.1890.

DUNVEGAN CASTLE DRAWINGS

NMRS Photographic Survey of drawings at Dunvegan Castle including designs for additions to Dunvegan Castle by Robert Brown 1840, etc.
Copied 1982 (NMRS Inventory 107).

DUNVEGAN ESTATE OFFICE DRAWINGS

NMRS Photographic Survey of Dunvegan Estate Office drawings copied per SRO including: survey plans of Dunvegan Castle by K and E Mackenzie 1920; design for improvements to Castle kitchens 1939; designs for restoration after fire of 24th November 1938 by Colin Simpson 1939; contract drawings for Dunvegan Hotel by Alexander Ross 1868; design for Dunvegan Village Hall 1894; designs for estate buildings and a survey of St Kilda by John Mathieson.
Copied 1979 (NMRS Inventory 107).

HENRY E EAST

(RIAS) Student notebooks with architectural and other sketches; notes from a lecture on 'Historical Architecture' and Certificates from the Department of Science and Art, 1896.

A small sketchbook, Insc.: 'Harry E East' '5 Erskine Terrace' with figure and architectural studies, including sketches of details of Lincoln Cathedral.

EASTEND HOUSE DRAWINGS

A small collection of designs by David Bryce 1855 and related documents, including an account by David Ness and Co. for chimney-pieces, and Letting particulars 1882.

EDENWOOD ALBUM

Photograph album with a survey of Edenwood House (Fife) and gardens, St Andrews, etc. c.1900.

EDINBURGH ARCHITECTURAL ASSOCIATION

The archive of the Edinburgh Architectural Association comprising incoming correspondence relating to visits, lectures, etc. and copy letter books of outgoing correspondence 1882–1908 (incomplete); lists of members 1885–1901; a box of material from the 1930s including correspondence, memoranda, press-cuttings, etc., on such concerns as the necessity for private practices to be allowed to compete for large public schemes; a large collection of EAA Syllabuses and those of related architectural societies; printed notices of meetings; a box of miscellaneous papers relating to architectural education.
On temporary deposit from the Edinburgh Architectural Association.

Illustrated Catalogue of Exhibition of Architectural Refinements, 1905

Exhibition Catalogue, 19 June to 10 August 1907. This exhibition at the Royal Scottish Academy marked the Jubilee of the EAA. The catalogue includes biographical details of architects whose portraits were exhibited.

(RIAS) Exhibition Catalogue, 1907. A large paper copy of the catalogue, with a photographic survey of the Jubilee Exhibition including portraits of 'deceased Scottish Architects', etc. Presented to EAA by Hippolyte Blanc, Chairman of the Exhibition Committee.

Xerox copies of nomination forms, bound

EDINBURGH ARCHITECTURAL
ASSOCIATION. Photographic survey of the
New Town of Edinburgh, Charlotte Square

EDINBURGH ARCHITECTURAL
ASSOCIATION. The entrance hall of
'Southgate' from 'Amateur House Decoration'

EDINBURGH ARCHITECTURAL
ASSOCIATION. Invitation card

alphabetically 1928–1933.
Originals with RIAS.

Xerox copy of W F Watson's *Edinburgh, its
Houses and Noted Inhabitants*, 1865. A
Catalogue to his collection prepared for a visit
by the EAA on the 8 May 1865. (Watson's
collection is now in the National Gallery of
Scotland.)
Original in National Library of Scotland.

John Marshall, *Amateur House Decorator*,
1883, being an illustrated version of a paper
read to the EAA 18 April 1883, describing the
decorations of D Marshall's Edinburgh villa,
'Southgate', Craigmillar Park.

Printed Library List, April 1905.

An album of press-cuttings recording the
activities of the Society, lectures, visits,
exhibitions, obituaries, etc., 2 November
1881–5 November 1907.
Purchased at sale of EAA Library.

Transactions, Vols. I–X, 1888–1930.

Xerox copy of George S Aitken's '*History and
Reminiscences of The Edinburgh Architectural
Association*, Typescript c.1911 with a
photograph of G S Aitken (architect and
founder-member of EAA) as frontispiece.
Original in RIAS Library.

Photographic survey of streets in the New
Town of Edinburgh. The prints of individual
buildings were mounted on boards and re-
photographed to complete street elevations.
This project was carried out in association with
the Edinburgh New Town Conservation
Committee by A L Hunter, Photography, and
the Photographic Department of RCAHMS.
The completed elevations were printed in
1971, and the mounted boards were
subsequently transferred to NMRS by the
RIAS in 1988.

EDINBURGH CALTON JAIL DRAWINGS

NMRS Photographic Survey of drawings in
Edinburgh City Architect's Department
including: designs for Calton Jail and
Bridewell by John Baxter 1791; designs for
alterations by Thomas Brown 1829; and
designs for Jedburgh Jail by Archibald Elliot
1820.
Copied 1971   (NMRS Inventory 28).

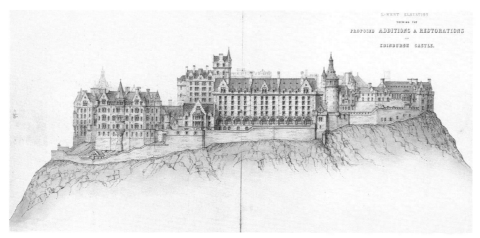

EDINBURGH CASTLE. Col. Moody's design for additions

EDINBURGH, CHAMBERS STREET. Cowgate, south side

EDINBURGH CASTLE

Portfolio. Design for 'Proposed Additions and Restorations'. Plan as existing, plans, elevations, perspectives and a 'Sketch of Principal Entrance Door to Edinburgh Castle'. These plans, drawn by Francis T Dollman 1859, accompanied Lt Col. Moody's Report for the Restoration of Edinburgh Castle.

EDINBURGH CASTLE ALBUM

Photograph album presented to Lord Napier recording the opening by Princess Louise of the restored Parliament Hall at Edinburgh Castle, with photographs before and after restoration and with oak boards, 1892.

EDINBURGH CASTLE, ST MARGARET'S CHAPEL

A file of historical notes and press-cuttings relating to its use for Presbyterian services 1932.

EDINBURGH, 32 CASTLE STREET, SIR WILLIAM FRASER'S COLLECTION

Photograph album recording the collection of early Scottish furniture formed by the celebrated Scottish genealogist, Sir William Fraser (1816–1898) and showing it arranged at 32 Castle Street, before its dispersal at auction by Dowells of Edinburgh on Saturday 3 December 1898.

EDINBURGH, CHAMBERS STREET

A collection of photographs recording this area, including the Cowgate, before the construction of the new streets. The photographs were probably taken for Sir William Chambers, c.1867.
From the collections of W and R Chambers.

EDINBURGH CITY ARCHITECT'S DRAWINGS COLLECTION

A large collection of 18th- and 19th-century drawings for public and private developments by the Magistrates of Edinburgh (one of the principal superiors in the development of the city) including: Royal High School by Thomas

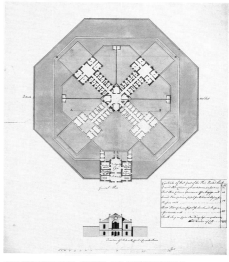

EDINBURGH CITY ARCHITECT'S DRAWINGS COLLECTION. Design for a Bridewell by John Baxter

26

Hamilton 1826; Scott Monument 1835–1871; North Bridge and North Bridge Street 1767–1771; Cockburn Street 1850–1880; Veterinary College, Clyde Street by R & R Dickson 1832; Pleasure Gardens and Winter Gardens, Princes Street 1849–1891; The Mound *c*.1815 and 1820; Inverleith Park 1888–1900; Calton Jail, unexecuted designs by John Baxter 1791; Leith Jail by Thomas Brown 1824; and schemes for Markets, Police Stations and Public Baths and Wash Houses.
Deposited by Technical Services Department, City of Edinburgh District Council, 1984.

EDINBURGH CITY MAPS

NMRS Photographic Survey of the collection of MS estate plans and printed maps formed by the City of Edinburgh, showing ownerships, proposed feuing lay-outs (e.g. 'Plan of Bearford's Parks by John Laurie, 1766') and including most of the standard later printed maps of the City and District.
Copied 1985. Originals on indefinite loan to the National Library of Scotland.

EDINBURGH, CORONATION ALBUMS

Two photograph albums with a survey of the temporary street and shop decorations erected in central Edinburgh to celebrate the Coronation of Edward VII, *c*.1902.

EDINBURGH, CORSTORPHINE PARISH CHURCH DRAWINGS

NMRS Photographic Survey of designs for Corstorphine Parish Church by Hay and Henderson 1892 and 1902; designs for proposed additions by Peddie and Kinnear 1890; and designs by William Young.
Copied 1971 and 1975   (NMRS Inventory 36).

EDINBURGH, FALCON HALL

A collection of photographs showing this Morningside villa and its grounds.
Presented by the Company of Merchants of the City of Edinburgh 1985.

EDINBURGH, FALCON HALL. Principal elevation

EDINBURGH, FETTES COLLEGE ALBUM

Photograph album with views of Fettes including a photograph taken 'after the fire of 1897'.

EDINBURGH, FETTES COLLEGE DRAWINGS

NMRS Photographic Survey of drawings for Fettes College including: Contract Drawings by David Bryce 1862 and 1864; designs for alterations by R Rowand Anderson 1883; designs for School Houses by R Rowand Anderson 1883, etc.
Copied 1974   (NMRS Inventory 60).

EDINBURGH, GRANTON GAS WORKS. Gasometer under construction

EDINBURGH, GRANTON GAS WORKS

Seventy-six photograph albums containing progress photographs of every aspect of architectural and technical construction undertaken by the Company at Granton including opening ceremony, etc. 1899–1931.

EDINBURGH, GEORGE HERIOT'S TRUST DRAWINGS

A large collection of 18th-century and 19th-century drawings relating to the Lands, Property and Buildings belonging to the Heriot Trust, one of the four important superiors in the development of the lands immediately north and west of the first New Town, including: Heriot Row by Robert Reid 1793–1803; Hampton Terrace and Victoria

EDINBURGH, GEORGE HERIOT'S TRUST DRAWINGS. Design for Coates Crescent

Villas 1851; Bangholm Cottages and Farm 1843–55; Eagles and Henderson's Nursery, Leith Walk 1849; Bellevue Place and Terrace 1856; Coates Farm 1846–1850; Palmerston Place 1875; Glencairn and Magdala Crescents 1869; Hillside Development, Leith Walk 1820–1823; Atholl Crescent 1825; and Hope Crescent by Robert Burn in 1825.
Deposited by George Heriot's Trust, 1984.

EDINBURGH, HIGHWAYS BOARD

A collection of plans for buildings in Edinburgh including: McDonald Road Electric Light Station 1903; Electric Light Station, Torphichen Street 1893; Shrubhill Power Station; Portobello Power Station Depot 1900; Music Hall, George Street 1899; sites for proposed statues including John Knox and Black Watch Memorial, Mound, 1909 and 1913; National Library of Scotland 1931; St Mary's Episcopal Cathedral 1874; Portobello Swimming Pool 1933; Meadowbank Power Station 1897; Boat House, Duddingston Loch 1898; Portobello Fever Hospital 1910, etc.

EDINBURGH, 'VIEWS OF HOLYROOD'

Album entitled 'Views of Holyrood', containing a comprehensive collection of engravings, lithographs, etc. of Holyrood Palace and Abbey c.1730–1850. Compiled c.1920 by the Hon. Sir Hew Hamilton-Dalrymple.

EDINBURGH, HOLYROOD ABBEY DRAWINGS

NMRS Photographic Survey of drawings for Holyrood Abbey in the collection of Ancient Monuments Branch, SDD, and now transferred to Scottish Record Office, including: survey drawing by James Gillespie Graham 1832; designs for restoration and additions by James Gillespie Graham and A W N Pugin 1837; and a set of working drawings for the restoration by James Gillespie Graham 1837.
Copied 1979   (NMRS Inventory 116).

EDINBURGH, LAURISTON CASTLE PHOTOGRAPH COLLECTION

NMRS Photographic Survey of the photograph collection of Mr and Mrs William Reid of Lauriston Castle, including: photographs of the premises of Morison and Co., Cabinetmakers, Edinburgh at 78 George Street; photographs of Mr and Mrs Reid's flat at 78 George Street 1894–1896; photographs of Lauriston Castle c.1910, etc.
Copied 1986.

EDINBURGH, 16 LEAMINGTON TERRACE, MATHER FAMILY ALBUM. Street elevation

EDINBURGH, 16 LEAMINGTON TERRACE, MATHER FAMILY ALBUM

Photograph album with a comprehensive survey of 16 Leamington Terrace c.1900, including exterior, interiors and gardens, showing the house as it was occupied by the family of Alexander Mather of Alexander

Mather and Son, Millwrights, Fountainbridge, Edinburgh.

EDINBURGH, J McKEAN'S PHOTOGRAPHS OF LEITH

Photograph album containing modern prints from c.1900 negatives of Leith views by J McKean, some of which have been reproduced in J Campbell Irons, *Leith and its Antiquities*, 1901.

OLD EDINBURGH PHOTOGRAPH ALBUM

Photograph album, Insc.: 'Old Edinburgh 1903–4' with 136 photographs by Robert Dykes, including: Edinburgh Castle; Holyrood; High Street and Canongate Closes; George Heriot's Hospital, etc.

EDINBURGH PHOTOGRAPHIC SOCIETY. Survey of George Square Ward

EDINBURGH PHOTOGRAPHIC SOCIETY

'Photographic Survey of Edinburgh and District' 'Ward XIV George Square', 81 mounts bearing labelled and dated photographs of buildings in this area (including names of photographers); mainly taken 1911–14, but including some earlier prints. The survey includes the monuments in Greyfriars Churchyard; the South side of the Lawnmarket; Lauriston; George Square, etc.
Purchased from Edinburgh Photographic Society by SNBR for £50, 1947.

EDINBURGH, PORTOBELLO

Album, containing proofs of 'Annals of Portobello' by William Baird. (Published as *Annals of Duddingston and Portobello*, 1898).

EDINBURGH, PORTOBELLO DRAWINGS

NMRS Photographic Survey of a collection of plans relating to Portobello including: designs for No. 67 Promenade, by Leadbetter and Smith 1863, and Charles Leadbetter 1873; designs for villas in John Street by Charles Leadbetter 1877; and a specification for a villa in John Street by Leadbetter and Smith 1863.
Copied 1978   (NMRS Inventory 114).

EDINBURGH: PROVISIONAL LIST OF BUILDINGS OF ARCHITECTURAL OR HISTORIC INTEREST

Provisional List of Buildings of Architectural or Historic Interest in Edinburgh, 1956–1958. Presented by C H Cruft.

EDINBURGH, ROYAL BOTANIC GARDEN LIBRARY DRAWINGS

NMRS Photographic Survey of Royal Botanic Garden drawings for the Physic Garden, Leith Walk, Edinburgh, and Inverleith, including: surveys by William Crawfurd 1777; survey by John Leslie 1763; design for a new Botanic Garden in Edinburgh by Sir James Nasmyth; sketch for a new Botanic Garden by Mr Crosbie, Advocate, and Mr Robertson, Architect; design for a Monument to Sir Charles Linnaeus by Robert Adam 1778 and James Craig *c*.1778; engraved plan of the Experimental Garden at Inverleith, etc.
Copied 1975   (NMRS Inventory 62).

EDINBURGH, ROYAL CRESCENT DRAWINGS

NMRS Photographic Survey of designs for Royal Crescent in Edinburgh City Architect's Department, including: Feuing Plan by Thomas Brown 1823 and elevations for houses by Thomas Brown 1826 and later; Feuing Plan

for ground west of Duncan Street by John Lessels 1881 and Feuing plan for ground east of Duncan Street by John Lessels 1883.
Copied 1973   (NMRS Inventory 51).

EDINBURGH, ROYAL EXCHANGE (CITY CHAMBERS) DRAWINGS

NMRS Photographic Survey of plans held by Edinburgh City Architect's Department, including; surveys and designs for alterations by the City Architects, David Cousin and Robert Morham 1854–1895.
Copied 1973   (NMRS Inventory 49).

EDINBURGH, THE ROYAL HIGH SCHOOL

Measured survey notes prepared by Charles Munro 1928–1929 for his measured drawings in NMRS.

Research notes, slides and photographs relating to Thomas Hamilton, Architect, and the Royal High School of Edinburgh compiled by J N McIsaac *c*.1960 and later.
Presented by J N McIsaac, 1990.

EDINBURGH, ST GEORGE'S CHAPEL, YORK PLACE DRAWINGS

NMRS Photographic Survey of design by James Adam 1792, and an album of photographs taken in November 1933.
Copied 1972   (NMRS Inventory 42).

EDINBURGH STREET FURNITURE

Research files prepared by Angus Graham, Secretary, RCAHMS, 1970.

EDINBURGH UNIVERSITY DEPARTMENT OF ARCHAEOLOGY

Field sheets, drawings, photographs and negatives, colour slides from pre-afforestation surveys sponsored by HBM/SDD in areas of Caithness and Sutherland, and the Bowmont Valley, Roxburghshire, 1976–1988; undertaken by the Department of Archaeology, University of Edinburgh, and directed by R J Mercer.

EDINBURGH, WALKER TRUST DRAWINGS

NMRS Photographic Survey of Walker Trust drawings including; plans of the Barony of Coates 1799 and 1802; feuing plan by James Gillespie Graham 1826; plans for Melville, Walker and Stafford Streets by Robert Brown 1820 and 1826; contract plans for Melville Crescent by John Watherston and Sons; elevation of Palmerston Place Church by Peddie and Kinnear 1874; and many individual house plans on estate presumably presented for approval by Trustees. (Drawings now in S.R.O.)
Copied 1979   (NMRS Inventory 10).

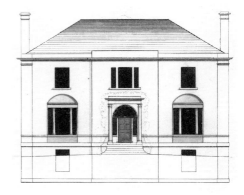

EDINBURGH, WARRISTON HOUSE (East). Elevation

EDINBURGH, WARRISTON HOUSE (East)

Portfolio. 'Plan of Andrew Bonar Esq House at Warriston 3, August 1808' Floor plans, elevations and sections attributed to Robert Burn.
Deposited on indefinite loan by Mrs Z Ashford, 1984.

EDINBURGH, JOHN WATSON'S SCHOOL DRAWINGS

NMRS Photographic Survey of drawings for John Watson's School, Edinburgh, including: designs by William Burn 1825–1828 including contract drawings; designs for the Gardener's House by John Watherston and Sons; Feuing plans for property owned by the Hospital at Ravelston, etc; by James Gillespie Graham 1819, David Bryce, John C Hay 1869, etc.
Copied 1979 (NMRS Inventory 97).

EDINBURGH, THE WEST BOW

A collection of sketchbooks including; a set of survey elevations (perhaps by John Henderson) prior to Thomas Hamilton's improvements to Edinburgh's Western Approaches, with list of property owners and historical notes; another with measured survey notes for properties in same area; the last with sketch elevations of carved tombstones in Arbroath and Dundee.
Society of Antiquaries of Scotland MSS 509.

EDINBURGH, WESTERN APPROACHES

A collection of designs for the Western Approaches to the City of Edinburgh by Thomas Hamilton, Architect, 1829–1830.
Society of Antiquaries of Scotland MSS (Purchased 1862).

EDMUNDSON'S ELECTRICITY CORPORATION LTD

Publicity Brochure. No date, c.1901 Broad Sanctuary Chambers, Westminster, London. With a list of commissions and photographic illustrations of electrified country houses, etc.
Purchased 1984.

ANDREW EDNIE, Architect and Designer

NMRS Photographic Survey of a collection of designs by Andrew Ednie dated from 1895–1905 in the possession of Glasgow Museums and Art Galleries. The collection includes survey sketches, measured drawings and designs. Many were prepared while he

was a student at the Edinburgh School of Applied Art.
Copied 1985.

DR FRANCIS EELES

Sketches from a dismembered sketchbook, 1891, including views and details of churches, etc., at: Arbuthnot; Beauly; Brechin; Cowie Chapel; Durris; Fortrose; Maryculter and Old Stonehaven.

Typescript Bibliography for the late Dr Francis Eeles, 1956.
Deposited by Miss Judith Scott, 1980 (NMRS Inventory 132).

ELDIN COLLECTION: JOHN CLERK OF ELDIN'S SALE CATALOGUE

Sale Catalogue (Contents) 16 Picardy Place, Edinburgh 14th March 1833 (Messrs Thomas Winstanley & Sons, Liverpool). Robert Adam's drawings were to be offered during this sale. Includes attached price list and 'A Concise and Accurate Acount of the Accident That Occurred at the Late Lord Eldin's Pictures' by a Sufferer (John Howell).

BURGH OF ELGIN DRAWINGS

NMRS Photographic Survey of drawings in possession of the Burgh of Elgin including: design for Court House and Jail 1837 (William Robertson); design for Court House and Jail 1832 (Archibald Simpson?); design for New Market 1848 (Thomas Mackenzie?); design for Elgin Gasworks 1846 and 1855; designs for restoration of the Bishop's House by R Rowand Anderson 1892 (two alternative schemes with a copy of accompanying letter to the Town Clerk).
Copied 1971 (NMRS Inventory 73).

DAVID ERSKINE SKETCHBOOK

NMRS Photographic Survey of a sketchbook by Sir David Erskine (1772–1837) including; Uphall House; Dryburgh Abbey; the Wallace Monument, Dryburgh; the Temple of the

Muses, Dryburgh; the Old Chain Bridge, Dryburgh; Dryburgh House; Melrose Market Cross; St Boswell's Green; Mertoun Parish Church; Cross at Layton, Bedfordshire; York Minster; Smailholm Tower; Comslie Tower; Landshaw Tower and Mill; and Branxholme Castle.
Copied 1978 (NMRS Inventory 98).

ESTATES EXCHANGE

Sale Catalogues. A collection transferred from NMR (England) 1983:

Allershaw	1905
Ardlussa, Jura	19.5.1901
Arnisdale	23.10.1919
Aros Castle	21.3.1918
Auchernach	14.5.1907
Auchmeddan	13.12.1898
do.	5.4.1918
Balgreggan	4.6.1902
Ballikinrain	24.7.1912
Barnaline	22.6.1916
Blair Drummond	21.6.1912
Bonawe	29.7.1914
Buness	3.4.1914
Carnsalloch	31.5.1911
Castle Semple	18.12.1907
Castle Toward	15.10.1919
Ceanacroc	21.10.1919
Craigengillan	30.4.1919
Cromar	9.1897
Drumtochty	28.10.1913
do.	12.9.1916
Duart Castle	14.7.1897
Dunalistair	23.10.1883
do.	24.6.1890
Dun Echt	15.6.1886
do.	31.7.1894
Dunnottar	14.5.1901
Ederline	24.5.1911
Faskally	15.7.1910
Foulden	4.4.1914
Freeland	5.11.1917
Freugh	4.6.1902
Galloway	18.12.1907
do.	11.7.1913
Gigha (Island)	26.7.1911
Glendaruel	7.6.1904
Glenrinnes	24.7.1917
Glen Tana	27.6.1907
Guisachan	16.6.1917

DUMFRIESSHIRE.

Carnsalloch Estate

1619·735 ACRES.   RENTS £2,578 3s. 2d.

TO BE SOLD BY AUCTION

By order of CAPTAIN A. F. CAMPBELL-JOHNSTON.

In the St. Mary's Hall, Dumfries, on Wednesday, May 31st, 1911, at 2 o'clock in the afternoon prompt.

Solicitors :—
Messrs. MACKENZIE & BLACK, W.S.,
28 Castle Street,
EDINBURGH.

Messrs. J. HENDERSON & SONS,
Solicitors,
DUMFRIES.

F. J. CASTIGLIONE & SONS,
Auctioneers and Land Agents,
THE COUNTY ESTATE OFFICES,
CARLISLE.

The Auctioneers will give orders to view the Estate.

ESTATES EXCHANGE. Sale Catalogue for Carnsalloch Estate

Hallmanor	1897
Haulkerton	5.8.1914
Inchdairnie	1907
Keithhall	6.8.1917
Kildalton and Oa	25.6.1914
Kilmahew	3.11.1919
Kinmount	14.10.1896
Kippilaw	30.4.1907
Lathrisk	25.8.1914
Lennel	7.1903
Lochnell	29.7.1914
Marchmont	24.6.1913
Menzies Castle	29.5.1914
Mertoun	16.7.1912
Mugdrum	16.7.1913
Nenthorn	7.7.1914
Netherley	14.5.1901
Orrok	5.3.1919
Penicuik	1894
Penningham	10.6.1919
Rachan	1894
Rannoch Lodge	11.7.1919
Ravenstone	2.6.1911
Rowallan	24.9.1901
St Martin's Abbey	1.2.1892

Strichen	13.12.1898
Symington Lodge	23.7.1913
Tarduf	3.7.1917
Taymouth Castle	9.12.1920
Tullichewan	7.4.1920
Westerhall	22.4.1911
do.	27.7.1911
Wiston	23.7.1913

THE FACTORS' SOCIETY

Photograph album containing portrait photographs of office-bearers and photographs taken during annual meetings and excursions, including Inverness, Balmoral, Blair Castle, Drummond Castle, Welbeck Abbey, Bolsover, Chatsworth and Clumber Park 1899–1904.
Presented by Mrs J S Townend.

DR HORACE FAIRHURST (1908–1986)

Excavation drawings, colour slides, photographs and negatives, correspondence and notes from surveys and excavations undertaken by Dr H Fairhurst 1936–72, including his major excavations at Crosskirk broch 1966–72.
Presented by Dr H Fairhurst and Mrs M Fairhurst.

J GRAHAM FAIRLEY (1846–1934), Architect

A small collection of personal papers including: Edinburgh Academy and Edinburgh University Engineering Class attendance tickets; *Le Salon*, 1922 with list of drawings exhibited by J Graham Fairley meriting an honourable mention; Salon exhibitor's admission ticket for 1922 with portrait photograph of J Graham Fairley; *Le Salon*, 1923 with list of drawings exhibited by J Graham Fairley awarded the 'Médaille Bronzé, and printed label indicating award; press-cuttings relating to works, interests and obituaries.
Deposited by his daughter, Miss J G Fairley.

REGINALD FAIRLIE (1883–1952), Architect

A collection of personal and business papers including: letters from R S Lorimer, G Gilbert Scott and John Scott to James Ogilvie Fairlie re his son Reginald's architectural training; sketch designs; photographs including St Benedict's Abbey, Fort Augustus; pamphlets relating to opening ceremonies, etc., including the opening of the National Library of Scotland; certificates and medals of the Royal Scottish Academy and framed exhibition panels for RSA exhibitions including: Dominican Convent, Hawick; Auchtermuchty War Memorial; and a Memorial Chapel for Falkland.
Presented by Captain D O Fairlie, 1984   (NMRS Inventory 154).

The office papers (drawings presumed destroyed) including: correspondence re

REGINALD FAIRLIE. Exhibition panel of the National Library, Edinburgh

National Library of Scotland 1933–1953; work for Sir John Stirling Maxwell at Pollok House and Corrour 1942–1947; a folder of drawings including a design for Melville House and a set of designs, Insc.: 'Leslie' dated 1778; correspondence with the Marquess of Bute *re* protection and purchase of historic buildings in Falkland, etc.; correspondence *re* the repair of the Kennedy Tomb, St Salvator's Church, University of St Andrews 1945–60; correspondence *re* Fort Augustus Abbey; exhibition drawings and photographs, including: the National Library of Scotland; St Nicholas House, St Leonard's School, St Andrews; Fort Augustus Abbey, etc.
Presented by A Conlon (Reginald Fairlie's partner).

FAST CASTLE AND DUNGLASS ESTATE

Research files relating to the history of Fast Castle and neighbourhood, Berwick District, 1985
Deposited by Mr K L Mitchell, 1985.

WILLIAM LEE FERGUSON

Nineteen sketchbooks. Many Insc.: 'William Lee Ferguson Duns 1900' and '1901', recording antiquarian subjects and Scottish historic architecture, mainly in the Borders, Edinburgh, Fife and Dumfries, with a few subjects in the North of England. The sketches dated '1900–1909'.
Presented to SNBR by F L Ferguson.

FETTERCAIRN DRAWINGS

NMRS Photographic Survey of designs for Fettercairn including: abstracts of architectural references from muniments; designs for additions to Colinton Castle, Edinburgh *c.*1800; designs for Colinton House by John Paterson 1801, Richard Crichton and Thomas Harrison *c.*1800–1803; designs for lodges and garden buildings at Invermay *c.*1800; designs for Dron Parish Church by William Stirling 1824; architectural drawings by James Forbes 18th century; and a large collection of designs for estate buildings. (Drawings now in the

National Library of Scotland).
Copied 1976 (NMRS Inventory 69).

J D FINLAYSON SKETCHBOOKS. Gosford Old House

J D FINLAYSON SKETCHBOOKS

Three sketchbooks of architectural and antiquarian subjects mainly in East Lothian, showing castles, villages, market crosses and doocots, many highly finished and with additional loose sketches. The earliest sketchbook dated 1893.
Presented to SNBR by his brother, William Finlayson, Redhouse, Longniddry, 1952.

J FLEMING

A collection of sketches from dismembered sketchbooks depicting tower houses and antiquarian subjects (one of Saddell Castle, Insc.: 'Sketched by John Fleming, 9 Woodside Crescent, Glasgow') and including Cassillis, Doune, Drochil, Dunnottar, Sauchie Old Tower, Stonebyres, etc., *c.*1900.

A A FOOTE AND SONS, Architects, Edinburgh

The Office Drawings: a large collection of designs for houses and commercial premises mainly in Edinburgh, but also including some war-time work in the Shetland Islands. The collection also includes a large number of exhibition panels comprising photographs and drawings 1928–1980.
Presented by A A Foote and Sons, 1981.

Job Book *c.*1928–1980
Presented by A A Foote and Sons

Miscellaneous papers of A A Foote and Son including Cash Book 1922–1947; Fee Book; souvenir brochures relating to opening of buildings designed by the firm; a design for a villa, 1862, 27 Buccleuch Street, Dumfries, and a printed circular regarding the price of Binny stone addressed to Robert Forrest, Sculptor, Calton Hill 1845.

MRS FOSTER FORBES OF ROTHIEMAY'S ALBUM. View of Ardmiddle House

MRS FOSTER FORBES OF ROTHIEMAY'S ALBUM

Photograph album 'presented to Mrs Foster Forbes of Rothiemay by the Members and Associates of the Turriff Branch of the Onward and Upward Association on the occasion of her leaving Dunlugas April 1892', with views of Dunlugas, Turriff, and neighbouring houses, including Ardmiddle, Forglen and Fyvie, etc.
Presented by Christies, South Kensington, 1988.

FORMANS AND McCALL ALBUM

Photograph album compiled by Charles de Neuville Forman (1852–1901) of Formans and McCall, Engineers, including engineering work, architectural subjects, bridges and portraits, (including Irvine Bridge, Darvel; Great Western Road Bridge, Glasgow;

Kelvindale Viaduct; West Highland Railway; 'The 1896 Holiday Habitation', etc).

JOHN FRAZER, Architect

(RIAS) A collection of student drawings by John Frazer, Edinburgh College of Art 1926–1931.

WILLIAM WALLACE FRISKIN (b.1889), Architect

A collection of personal papers and exhibition drawings by William Friskin including school and Glasgow School of Architecture certificates 1905–1910; honourable mention for RIBA's Soane Medallion 1912; letters home while on active service in France 1916–1918; certificates of membership, Incorporation of Architects in Scotland 1922 and RIAS 1943; medals including: Excellence in architectural design, Glasgow School of Art 1908 and 'Past President', Dundee Institute of Architects 1945–47; portraits by his wife, L Friskin 1948; exhibition drawings for houses designed by Friskin, including a block of flats in Montevideo and a house at Pitlochry 1952, etc.
Presented by the executors of William Friskin, 1987, per Mrs E Beattie.

T BOWHILL GIBSON (c.1895–1949), Architect

(RIAS) The office drawings.

JAMES GILES (1801–1870), Artist

NMRS Photographic Survey of James Giles' drawings of Aberdeenshire Castles undertaken for the Earl of Aberdeen 1839–58 and now in the collection of the National Trust for Scotland, including: Castle Fraser, Fyvie, Huntly, Monymusk, Pitsligo, Skene, Towie Barclay, etc.
Copied 1988 (NMRS Inventory 168).

JAMES GILLESPIE, Architect (Ministry of Public Buildings and Works, Edinburgh)

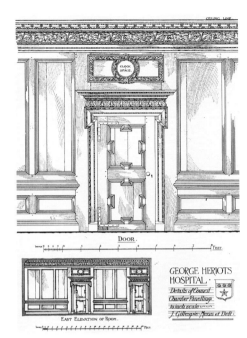

JAMES GILLESPIE. Record drawing of Council Chamber, George Heriot's Hospital, Edinburgh

A collection of measured survey drawings prepared as plates for James Gillespie's *Details of Scottish Domestic Architecture*, including Rowallan Castle; Midhope Castle; Riddle's Court, Edinburgh; Cowane's Hospital, Stirling; Pilmuir House; Kelburn Castle; Trade's House, Aberdeen; Winton Castle; Traquair House; Kinross House; and Pollok House, etc.

JAMES GILLESPIE (1854–1914) AND JAMES SCOTT (1861–1944), Architects

Xerox copy of Job Book, 1889–1978.

EWING GILMOUR ALBUM

Photograph album, Insc.: 'Views on Gilmour Estates Ross and Sutherland' c.1910, including

Armadale Lodge, Eriboll Lodge, Rosehall House and Estate, and Strathkyle Lodge.

GLASGOW CATHEDRAL DRAWINGS

NMRS Photographic Survey of a collection of drawings for Glasgow Cathedral in the collection of Ancient Monuments Branch, SDD, and now transferred to SRO, including: survey drawings by James Gillespie Graham; designs for additions attributed to A W N Pugin, 1837; plan and section by Robert Matheson 1850; elevations showing arrangements of monumental tablets by Edward Blore 1850; designs for stained glass by C H Wilson; and a survey of the Mynto Monument by George R Baird 1915.
Copied 1979 (NMRS Inventory 116).

GLASGOW, THE EMPIRE EXHIBITION ALBUM 1938

Photograph album with amateur snapshots of the Empire Exhibition, Glasgow 1938.

A file of press photographs with general views and details of pavilions.

GLASGOW INTERNATIONAL EXHIBITION 1901

Photograph album with amateur snapshots of the Exhibition and Pavilions.

GLASGOW, MADEIRA COURT BUILDINGS

Portfolio. Set of lithographed plans, Insc.: 'John Burnet, Architect, 113 West Regent Street, Glasgow' of the 'Madeira Court Buildings, the property of George Martin Esq.' and bearing Burnet's stamp inside front cover. c.1870.

GLASGOW, TEMPLETON'S CARPET FACTORY DRAWINGS

NMRS Photographic Survey of Drawings in Glasgow Dean of Guild Collection including: designs by George A Boswell 1936 for new factory, Glasgow Green; design for new

premises at Templeton Street by Geo. A
Boswell 1927; extension to Templeton Street
Factory by Geo. A Boswell 1934, etc.
Copied 1980   (NMRS Inventory 77).

NMRS Photographic Survey of designs for
Templeton's Carpet Factory in the possession
of British Carpets Ltd, including designs for
new factory by William Leiper (Doge's Palace,
62 Templeton Street, Glasgow) 1888 and copy
of a list of drawings in the plan store.
Copied 1979   (NMRS Inventory 91).

ESME GORDON, Architect (*b*.1910)

(RIAS) A collection of exhibition drawings by
Esme Gordon, including: designs for the South
of Scotland Electricity Board Headquarters,
George Street, Edinburgh 1961; designs for St
Giles' Cathedral, Edinburgh 1951, etc.
Presented by Esme Gordon.

ISOBEL GORDON, Architect

(RIAS) A collection of drawings by Isobel
Gordon while she was a student at Robert
Gordon's College, School of Architecture,
Aberdeen 1929–1933.

ANGUS GRAHAM (1892–1979)

Angus Graham was Secretary of the Royal
Commission between 1935 and 1957; this
material in the RCAHMS collection includes
his fieldwork notebooks, other notebooks,
photograph albums showing sites and
monuments throughout Britain and Ireland
1936–49, and index cards containing notes and
descriptions used to compile his paper 'Some
Observations on the Brochs' published in the
*Proceedings of the Society of Antiquaries of
Scotland.*

Mss Diary June 1st 1934—31st December
1968; articles on forestry subjects; portrait
photographs and obituaries, and proof copy of
an appreciation and bibliography by J G
Dunbar *PSAS*, 111 (1981), pp. 1–6.

GRAHAMSTON IRON CO. LTD

Catalogue of Rainwater and Soil Goods. No
date, *c*.1950. Falkirk.
Presented by SRO 1987.

WALTER GORDON GRANT (1886–1947)

Copies of a collection of drawings by David
Wilson of Grant's excavation on Rousay,
Orkney, between 1929 and 1946. The original
drawings are housed in Tankerness House
Museum, Kirkwall, Orkney.

GREENOCK, DRUMFROCHAR ROAD, WORSTED MILLS

A collection of plans for the Worsted Mills,
Drumfrochar Road, Greenock, by James
Houston, *c*.1953, etc.
*Presented per Mr W Graham, L Jowett and
Co., Merino Industrial Estate, Greenock,
1988.   (NMRS Inventory 169).*

*GRIBLOCH COLLECTION. Model for
Gribloch House*

GRIBLOCH COLLECTION

A large collection of designs, photographs,
correspondence, and a model for Gribloch
House designed by Sir Basil Spence for John
Colville 1937–1938. Includes correspondence
with contractors including: Gordon Russell,
Betty Joel, Charles Henshaw, Green and
Abbot, etc. A number of other designers were
involved, including Perry Duncan and
Raymond Subes.
*Deposited by Lady Hutchison, daughter of
John Colville, 1990.*

J SYMINGTON GRIEVE (*d*.1932)

Collection of notebooks with sketches,
photographs and negatives reflecting
Symington Grieve's interest in the archaeology
and natural history of Argyll (in particular,
Colonsay and Oronsay, 1913–25). Some of this
material may have been used for Grieve's
publication *The Book of Colonsay and
Oronsay*, 1923.

THOMAS HADDEN. Fire irons

THOMAS HADDEN, Decorative Ironworker and Smith

A large collection of negatives illustrating
work by this firm, who were extensively
employed by Sir Robert Lorimer for gates,
railings, grates, fire-irons, etc. The majority of
the items were photographed in the studio and
are thus unidentified and have no context
c.1900–1930.
Presented by R M Hadden, 1979.

HADDO HOUSE AND ESTATE DRAWINGS

NMRS Photographic Survey of drawings at Haddo House including: designs for alterations by Archibald Simpson 1827; designs for alterations by Wardrop and Reid 1879–1880; designs for interior details by Wright and Mansfield (1880); designs for the Chapel at Haddo House by G E Street 1879; proposed rearrangement of South wing by George Bennett Mitchell and Son 1930; and many designs for churches, farm buildings, etc., on estates.
Copied 1969   (NMRS Inventory 14).

DAVID HAMILTON (1768–1843), Architect

Photostat set of his drawings formerly in the Glasgow Philosophical Society and now in Glasgow University Library (Bound in four volumes with index).

JOHN R C HAMILTON (1917–1985)

J R C Hamilton excavated at two of Scotland's most important sites, Jarlshof settlement 1949–52 and Clickhimin broch and settlement 1954–57, while with the Inspectorate of Ancient Monuments. This collection contains a few of the original excavation drawings, photographs, notebooks and correspondence, and comprises mainly the secondary publication material.

HAMILTON DRAWINGS

NMRS Photographic Survey of Hamilton Drawings including: designs for Hamilton Palace 1693–1695 by J Smith and J Smith; designs for plasterwork at Hamilton Palace by Thomas Clayton 1746–52; designs for Hamilton Palace 1811 and 1816; designs for Hamilton Palace by Francesco Saponieri (Naples) 1819 and Charles Percier 1828–29; designs and working drawings for Hamilton Palace by David Hamilton 1820s and 1830s; designs for decorations by Robert Hume 1840s; designs for the Mausoleum at Hamilton by H E Goodridge 1846, David Hamilton 1841 and David Bryce 1848–1851; many record drawings of celebrated historic buildings in Italy; designs for Strabane House, Arran by George Paterson 1883; designs for additions to

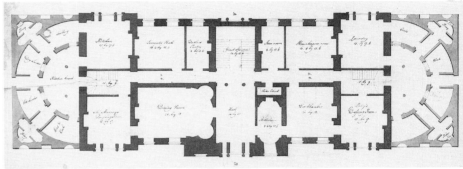

HANGINGSHAW HOUSE. Design for Hangingshaw House by James Adam

Lennoxlove in 1801 and 1825; designs for additions to Lennoxlove by William Burn 1823 and Sydney Mitchell and Wilson 1913–1914; and a design for the restoration of Kinneil House by R S Lorimer 1909, etc.
Copied 1971 and 1979   (NMRS Inventory 32).

HAMILTON PALACE

Sale Catalogue (Contents) June 17 1882, Christie, Manson and Woods, London. Photographically illustrated.

Sale Catalogue (Contents) *Illustrated Priced Catalogue* June 17 1882 Librairie de l'Art, Paris: Remington and Co, London. Souvenir Catalogue. Illustrated with engravings.

Sale Catalogue. *Remaining Contents and Demolition Materials* Wednesday 12 November 1919 Christie, Manson and Woods. On the premises. Photographically illustrated and with a history by H Avray Tipping (after *Country Life*).

HANGINGSHAW HOUSE

(RIAS) A portfolio of designs, Insc.: 'House for John Murray Esq of Philiphaugh' S. and d. 'James Adam Archt. 1768'.

REV. W FERGUS HARRIS COLLECTION OF PHOTOGRAPHS

NMRS Photographic Survey of a large collection of Scottish architectural photographs in the possession of the Rev. W Fergus Harris, which may have been used by MacGibbon and Ross in the preparation of their histories of

Scottish Architecture. (The photographs are now in NMRS).
Copied 1973 (NMRS Inventory 47).

DAVID HARVEY, Architect

A small collection of miscellaneous personal and architectural papers including a photographic portrait; a receipt from David Harvey, Grocer, Leith 1908; a report from Daniel Stewart's College, Edinburgh 1924–1925; photographs of finished drawings for student projects, including the design for a Scottish National Library and a proposed high level Street, Princes Street–Leith Walk, Edinburgh; an isometric drawing of a grain elevator at Leith 1932; competition entry for Newcastle-upon-Tyne Town Hall; a photograph of the neon-lit balustrade at the National Bank of Scotland, 9–11 George Street, Edinburgh c.1939; wartime papers and later wedding invitations, birth notices for members of family, etc. (Found at his house in Lanark Road, Edinburgh).
Presented by Elizabeth Strong, 1987.

HATTON CASTLE DRAWINGS

NMRS Photographic Survey of drawings at Hatton Castle including designs for a Mausoleum (probably by Alexander Reid of Elgin 1861) and miscellaneous plans for lodges and seating at Turriff Parish Church 1864.
Copied 1967   (NMRS Inventory 23).

HATTON HOUSE

Album. Extra-illustrated copy of J R Findlay, *Hatton House*, 1875, including additional photographs, original drawings by James Drummond, RSA, (used as woodcuts in the text), proofs of the woodcuts and an 18th-century engraving of the house after Slezer. This was J R Findlay's own copy with his bookplate, and it has been especially bound with a die on the cover taken from the monogram on the West Pavilion.

HATTON HOUSE. Album: the drawing room with Mrs J R Findlay

HAWICK MUSEUM DRAWINGS

NMRS Photographic Survey of a large collection of drawings at Hawick Museum including: designs for Teviot Mills; Weensland Mills; Waverley Mills; Feuing plan for Kirkhill; designs for the Buccleuch Memorial, Hawick; Langland Mills; and Hawick Slaughter House mid 19th Century–20th Century.
Copied 1975   (NMRS Inventory 63).

KATE HAWKINS (1896–1989), Garden designer

A collection of papers relating to the design of gardens throughout Scotland by Kate Hawkins, including correspondence, account books, etc., 1950s–1980s
Presented per the Garden History Society.

A D HAXTON, Architect

The Office Drawings. A very large collection of designs for farms, housing, commercial premises, etc., mainly in Fife, designed by this architect, based in Leven. During the 1930s

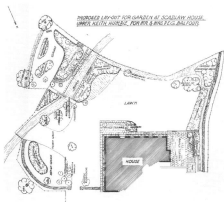

KATE HAWKINS. Design for Scadlaw House Gardens

the firm specialised in cinemas and carried out a number of projects in central Scotland, and the collection includes many drawings by subcontractors, e.g. for neon lighting schemes, etc.
Presented by the successor to A D Haxton.

HAXTON AND WATSON, Architects

Photocopy of Job Book arranged by running number and by building types, e.g. 'Housing' and 'Cinemas' c.1963.

GEORGE HAY (1911–1987), Architect

MS copy of '*Scottish Architectural Woodwork of the Sixteenth and Seventeenth Centuries*', submitted as thesis for RIBA final examination, 1936; illustrated with photographs and measured drawings.
Presented by Dr George Hay.

Survey plans of Scottish Churches prepared for plates in George Hay, *The Architecture of the Post Reformation Church in Scotland*, 1957.
Presented by Dr George Hay, 1981.

HEBRIDEAN NEWSCUTTING ALBUMS

Two albums. One Insc.; 'Hebridean News Cuttings 1950.51. 52. 53 Volume I W A Shand' covering life in the Hebrides. The second, (covered in Harris tweed) compiled to give a picture of life in the islands, history, religion, the development of local housing-patterns, etc., and including several especially taken photographs.
Presented by Miss W A Shand.

HELENSBURGH, CROMALT HOUSE

Five Photograph albums showing exterior, grounds and interiors of Cromalt House during the lifetime of Neil Munro.
Presented by Ian Gow.

HENDERSON COLLECTION. Design for Borthwick Hall

JOHN HENDERSON (1804–1864), Architect and GEORGE HENDERSON (1846–1905) of HAY AND HENDERSON, Architects

A large collection of designs and photographs by both father and son including: sketch designs; presentation drawings; a sketchbook by George Henderson of medieval ecclesiastical detail, 1863; exhibition drawings; photographs and source material. The John Henderson collection includes many designs for churches throughout Scotland, particularly for the Episcopal Church. Representative examples are the drawings for Holy Trinity Episcopal Church, Edinburgh, 1838 and the large set (including presentation and contract

HISTORIC BUILDINGS AND MONUMENTS (SDD). Sketewan, Perthshire, excavation by R J Mercer

drawings) for the private Episcopal Chapel at Ardgowan for Sir Michael Shaw Stewart 1854. The George Henderson Collection includes some drawings, but mainly photographs of the extension by Hay and Henderson of Old St Paul's Church, Edinburgh 1888–1892, and of George Henderson's work at Bermuda Cathedral 1885. The drawings date from c.1836 to 1900.
Deposited by the executors of the late Mrs Stella Phillipps, daughter of George Henderson.

THE HIRSEL DRAWINGS

NMRS Photographic Survey of drawings at the Hirsel including: design for a Memorial Cross at Douglas by A N Paterson 1918; sketch surveys of the Hirsel 1813; designs for the Hirsel by Edwin Lutyens 1886; designs for additions by Wardrop and Reid 1882–1883; designs for additions by James C Walker 1885; portfolio of designs for additions to Douglas Castle by James Playfair 1791; survey of Bothwell Castle by R Rowand Anderson 1886; and designs for decoration at the Hirsel by Owen Jones 1872.
Copied 1980 (NMRS Inventory 122).

HISTORIC BUILDINGS AND MONUMENTS (SCOTTISH DEVELOPMENT DEPARTMENT)

The largest single external collection of archaeological material relates to the excavations and surveys funded and sponsored by Historic Buildings and Monuments (HBM/SDD), or the previous equivalent government departments: the Inspectorate of Ancient Monuments in the SDD, the

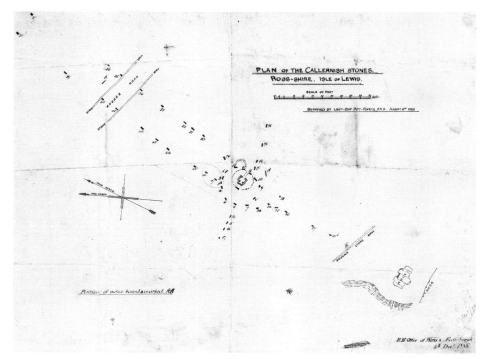

*HISTORIC BUILDINGS AND
MONUMENTS (SDD). General Pitt Rivers'
survey of Callanish, Ross and Cromarty*

Department of the Environment (DOE), the
Ministry of Works (MoW), and the Office of
Works. The collection is added to annually
and comprises a wide range of material
(including original excavation and survey
notebooks, drawings, photographs and
negatives), extending from a General Pitt
Rivers drawing of Callanish 1885, for the
Office of Works, to records of the most recent
excavations undertaken by Archaeological
Operations and Conservation (AOC), formerly
the Central Excavation Unit (CEU), the
survey and excavation wing of HBM.

A large collection of glass negatives, recording
Scheduled Ancient Monuments and those in
Guardianship, transferred to NMRS in 1986.
*(NMRS Inventory 166; with concordance of
previous HBM negative numbers).*

A large collection of modern negatives
showing buildings Listed as category 'C', taken
during re-Listing in the late 1970s and a large
collection of negatives of buildings considered
for Listing by HBM in the 1960s–1980s.

HENRY HOPE AND SONS

Plans and Photographs of 15 Cottages.
1920. Smethwick, Staffordshire.
Designs utilising Hope's Standard Steel
Windows by Lutyens, Lorimer, etc.
Purchased 1981.

HOPETOUN DRAWINGS

NMRS Photographic Survey of a collection of
drawings found in the Laundry at Hopetoun
House in the 1960s, including: designs for

alterations, new safe, etc., by Rowand
Anderson and Paul 1904; Engineers' drawings
by Glyde, Chaffey and Co. 1910; and many
designs for estate buildings 1877–1904.
Copied 1985   (NMRS Inventory 146).

ERIC J HOSIE

Typescript copies of research notes and draft
histories of Bothwell Castle, Culzean Castle,
and Dunglass Castle, 1966–1968.

HOUSE OF SCHIVAS

Press-cuttings, photographs and letters from
1st Baron Catto to J Fenton Wyness,
Architect, concerning their restoration of
House of Schivas 1932–1942. Includes a
miniature sketchbook by J Fenton Wyness (9
May 1903) with a sketch survey of Lorimer's
Craigmyle House.
*Passed to NMRS, per Mr C T Burnett, the
National Museums of Scotland, 1986.*

J & R HOWIE LTD

Catalogue of Fireclay Drainage Materials: tiles,
chimneys, sanitary ware, garden ornaments.
1954. Hurlford Fireclay Works, Kilmarnock.
Presented by SRO, 1987.

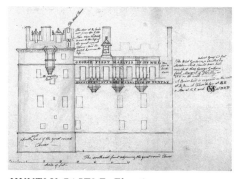

HUNTLY CASTLE. Elevation

HUNTLY CASTLE

A portfolio of record drawings with survey plans and elevations, and details of ornaments c.1816.

ALEXANDER HUTCHISON ALBUM. The business room at 10 York Place

ALEXANDER HUTCHISON ALBUM

Photograph album, Insc.: 'Photographs by Alexander Hutchison (1840–1924) of 17 Dublin Street, Edinburgh', cabinetmaker and amateur photographer. Includes views of Maxpoffle; Craigmillar Castle; Duddingston; Abbotsford; Gilmerton House; Darnick Tower; 7 and 9 Drummond Place, Edinburgh; 10 York Place, Edinburgh; 6 and 10 Bellevue Crescent; and two views of the meeting room of the 'Monks of St Giles' c.1910.

INCHINNAN AIRSHIP SHED DRAWINGS

A collection of designs for Inchinnan Airship Shed by Sir W M Arrol and Co. 1915–1917. *Presented by Sir William Arrol, 1987 (NMRS Inventory 167).*

INGLIS COLLECTION

See Scottish Colorfoto Limited.

INNES PHOTOGRAPH COLLECTION

A large collection of photographs by D Innes, Lysvold, Currie, of Scottish subjects, many taken to illustrate both his articles and those of his wife, Agnes, in *Scotland's Magazine*, etc. 1950s.

INVENTORY OF GARDENS AND DESIGNED LANDSCAPES IN SCOTLAND

Research files compiled by Land Use Consultants during their preparation of the 'Inventory of Gardens and Designed Landscapes in Scotland', sponsored by the Countryside Commission for Scotland and Historic Buildings and Monuments, SDD. The files are arranged by region and then alphabetically by garden name. (N.B. Many files are on closed access and may only be consulted after obtaining the owner's permission.) A collection of photographs taken during survey work. The conclusions were published as *An Inventory of Gardens and Designed Landscapes in Scotland*, 1987. *Deposited by the sponsoring bodies, 1987.*

INVERARAY CASTLE DRAWINGS

NMRS Photographic Survey of drawings for Inveraray Castle including: designs by Dugal Campbell before 1743, Roger Morris 1745–1747, Robert Mylne 1777–1780, Joseph Bonomi 1806; driveway design by W A Nesfield 1848; designs for additions by Anthony Salvin post 1877; designs for estate buildings including bridges; designs for Inveraray Town, including Town House by John Adam 1754; designs for a circular Church by John Adam 1760; designs for Inveraray Parish Church by Robert Mylne 1800; design for Ardkinglas by Colen Campbell early 18th century; design for Inveraray Manse 1842; designs for Inveraray Court House by Robert Reid 1807; designs for restoration of Inveraray Castle by Ian G Lindsay 1951–1966; designs for Inveraray Town by Robert Mylne c.1786; survey by William Boutcher 1721; and many designs for estate buildings, Campbeltown, etc. *Copied 1973, 1975 (NMRS Inventory 72).*

INVERNESS TOWN HOUSE DRAWINGS

NMRS Inventory of drawings in Inverness Town House. Listed 1976.

IONA ALBUM. Sketch view of the Abbey

IONA

Album, Insc.: 'Drawings and Sketches of Tombs and other matters In the Island of Iona; done in 1848 and 1849 the greater portion of which have been published under the Name of 'The Antiquities of Iona 1850' 'By Henry D Graham. Gent. resident in the Island'. Comprising topographical sketches, record drawings of the monuments and carved stones, and sketches of archaeological finds. With accompanying texts interleaved. Several of the sketches are unpublished. *Presented by Miss Iona Chatterton (granddaughter of Henry D Graham), 1988.*

IONA ABBEY

Manuscript lecture, Insc.: 'Lecture on the Architecture of the Abbey Church of St Mary Iona', attributed to John Watson c.1900.

IONA ALBUM, ANCIENT TOMBS

Photograph album, Insc.: 'Photographs of Ancient Tombs Iona', containing a photographic survey of carved grave slabs on Iona. Photographs by the Revd. J Mackenzie of Colonsay 1870s. Possibly produced as a limited edition.

JAMES THOMAS IRVINE

A collection of letters to and from J T Irvine relating to various architectural researches, and his covering letter donating them to the Society of Antiquaries of Scotland Library 1863–1897.
Society of Antiquaries of Scotland MSS 617.

ISLAY, LAPHROAIG DISTILLERY DRAWINGS

NMRS Photographic Survey of plans for Laphroaig Distillery including: survey drawings by William Gemmil 1840 and engineers' drawings by John Norman and Co. 1870.
Copied 1980 (NMRS Inventory 117).

CHARLES d'O PILKINGTON JACKSON (1887–1973), Sculptor

Three photograph albums covering travels in Italy and Egypt with commercial art photographs and his own snapshots *c*.1900–1910.

Manuscript and draft typescript of Pilkington Jackson's history of the carved wooden statuettes of Scottish soldiers made for the Scottish Military Museum conceived as an adjunct to the Scottish National War Memorial 1928–1933.

MAGNUS JACKSON, Photographer, Perth

NMRS Photographic Survey printed from negatives taken by Magnus Jackson of architectural subjects (castles, country houses, and villages), mainly in Perthshire, including Taymouth Castle *c*.1880; Pitfour Castle *c*.1880; villas in Crieff, etc.
Printed 1966–1970.

J JERDAN AND SON (*c*.1841–1913), Architects

(RIAS) A collection of exhibition drawings by John Jerdan and exhibition photographs illustrating commissions executed by this firm including: Davaar House, Earlsferry;

GEORGE PENROSE KENNEDY. Design for remodelling Drummond Castle

Chisholme House, Roxburghshire; Benarty House, Colinton; Prestonkirk Reredos; Edenhall Hostel; Templehall House; the restoration of White Horse Close, Canongate, Edinburgh; and several unidentified *c*.1903–1914.

THOMAS JOHNSTON, Antiquarian

An antiquarian notebook compiled by Thomas Johnston, describing archaeological sites and castles, etc. in South West Scotland *c*.1826. A transcript of Ewart of Mullock's Monument of 1642 by William Johnston (brother of Thomas). A letter from the Society of Antiquaries of London to Thomas Johnston 18.12.1826 thanking him for the 'fragments' and encouraging him in his researches.
Society of Antiquaries of Scotland   MSS 371.

ALEXANDER KEILLER (1889–1955)

This collection represents Keiller's major involvement in Scottish archaeology and comprises survey drawings, notebooks and a few photographs. Keiller described and surveyed numerous stone circles in North East Scotland in the 1920s, before moving to Wiltshire, where he excavated at Windmill Hill, Avebury, and the West Kennet Avenue.
Presented by Professor S Piggott.

KEIR DRAWINGS

NMRS Photographic Survey of drawings for Keir House and estates including: designs for Keir by David Hamilton 1829–30; designs by Alfred Jenure 1849–50; designs by William Jenure 1849–50; designs for additions by Sir Rowand Anderson 1902–1905; and designs for estate buildings.
Copied 1975   (NMRS Inventory 64).

GEORGE MEIKLE KEMP (1795–1844), Architect

(RIAS) A collection of drawings relating to his design for the Scott Monument, Edinburgh, including studies after Melrose, unfinished working drawings, etc.

GEORGE PENROSE KENNEDY (*fl*.1830— after 1868), Architect

A small collection of designs for additions to Drummond Castle.
Purchased 1980, when the Kennedy Albums were broken up and auctioned by Sothebys.

HENRY KERR (1854–1946), Architect

A collection of eight identical notebooks, one Insc.: 'Henry F Kerr, 62 Hanover Street, Edinburgh' devoted to various subjects and indexed at the rear. The subjects include: 'Farm Buildings', 'Byzantine Architecture';

two volumes 'Scottish History'; church furniture; heraldry and two on miscellaneous architectural subjects including squash courts, kitchens, etc.; and one with copy plans, elevations and views of houses and cottages admired by Kerr, including works by Lorimer, etc. (Kerr had compiled a list of historic architectural records for SNBR).
Purchased with much of his Library by SNBR 1946.

(RIAS) 'Henry Kerr's Photograph Collection'. A large collection of prints and negatives believed to have belonged to Henry Kerr, including some commercial views, but mainly taken on the outings of the Edinburgh Architectural Association c.1900–1910 or relating to publications in the EAA *Transactions*. Includes: Aberdour Castle; Argyll Lodging, Stirling; Balbardie; The Binns; Bo'ness; Caerlaverock; Caroline Park, Edinburgh; Chatelherault; Claypotts; Craigievar; Crathes; Culross Abbey House; Dalquharran Castle; Drumlanrig; Dundas Castle; Dunglass Church; Falkland Palace; Fordell Castle; Fyvie; Gosford; Hamilton Palace; Holyroodhouse; Inverkeithing; Kinross House; Linlithgow Palace; Mars Work, Stirling; Melrose Abbey; Midhope Castle; Newark Castle; Northfield House; Pinkie House; Pitreavie; Pittencrieff; Pollok Castle; 68 and 69 Queen Street, Edinburgh; Rowallan Castle; St Bridget's Church; Thirlestane Castle; Udny Castle, and Winton House.

LEWIS KIDD?

Album containing a variety of sketches, tracings and cuttings of antiquarian and modern furniture, e.g. Great Bed of Ware and bed at Crathes; an étagère, Insc.: 'Edinburgh design'; lithographed priced chair designs; a watercolour design for a Carolean chair with twisted uprights; and sketches showing flower borders at Gordon Castle, (one Insc.: 'Lewis Kidd 1844'; a summer house at Monaltrie, etc. Paper watermarked '1822'.

KILKERRAN DRAWINGS

NMRS Photographic Survey of drawings for Kilkerran including: plans for alterations

LEWIS KIDD? Album: design for a whatnot made in Edinburgh

c.1740; portfolios of designs by James Gillespie (Graham) 1813 and 1818; designs for proposed Billiards Room by David Bryce 1855; design for new presses in library 1833; designs for additions by Brown and Wardrop 1873 and 1875.
Copied 1975 (NMRS Inventory 61).

KIMMERGHAME DRAWINGS

NMRS Photographic Survey of drawings at Kimmerghame including: design for a house attributed to William Chambers 1770; designs for Kennet House by Thomas Harrison 1793–1794; 18th-century plans for altering Kimmerghame House; designs for Broadmeadows 1804–1805; designs for Broadmeadows by David Hamilton 1811; designs for new house and lodges by William Burn 1827; and designs and contract drawings for the executed house by David Bryce 1853.
Copied 1969 (NMRS Inventory 27).

KINFAUNS CASTLE DRAWINGS

A collection of drawings for Kinfauns Castle and estate including: plan of the pantry and plate room 1815; design for the gas house by James Milne and steam engine 1825 and 1828; designs for stables and farm buildings by Robert Smirke 1826; designs for lodges 1821–1924; design for a stained glass window, Insc.: 'Mr Gillespie'; and designs for proposed additions by Robert Smirke 1831.
Presented after discovery in Factor's House.

KINLOCH HOUSE PLANS

NMRS Photographic Survey of plans at Kinloch House including: plans by 'G K 1797' (probably George Kinloch, the then owner); an elevation of 1798; plans for a new house c.1800; and plans for proposed alterations by John Carver, Kinloch 1864.
Copied 1969 (NMRS Inventory 16).

KINLOCHMOIDART HOUSE DRAWINGS

NMRS Photographic Survey of drawings for Kinlochmoidart House including: a set of unexecuted designs by William Leiper, January 1883, and an estate survey c.1800 with a vignette of the house.
Copied 1987 (NMRS Inventory 164).

KINNAIRD CASTLE DRAWINGS

NMRS Photographic Survey of drawings for Kinnaird including: a bound volume of plans for Kinnaird by Sir William Bruce and Alexander Edward 1695–1698 and John Slezer, and designs for additions by David Bryce 1853–1855.
Copied 1976 (NMRS Inventory 67).

KINNORDY HOUSE DRAWINGS

NMRS Photographic Survey of drawings at Kinnordy including: alternative designs for Inverquharity Castle by Wardrop and Reid 1878 and plans for surveys and designs for Kinnordy 1823–1850.
Copied 1969 (NMRS Inventory 12).

MANDERSTON:
FOR SIR JAS: P. MILLAR BART
TEA ROOM OVER
DAIRY AT BUXLEY

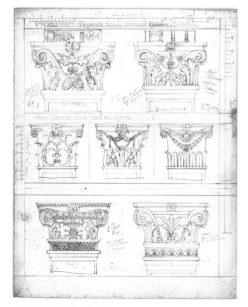

JOHN KINROSS. Design for the dairy at Manderston and details from Italian buildings

HARRY BEDFORD LEMERE. View of the window seat at Hill House, Helensburgh designed by Charles Rennie Mackintosh

JOHN KINROSS (1855–1931), Architect

(RIAS) A collection of sketches, preparatory and finished drawings for plates in John Kinross, *Details from Italian Buildings*, 1882. *Peter Miller Collection.*

Exhibition drawings for the Royal Scottish Academy, 'Greyfriars Elgin, For the Most Honble. The Marquess of Bute', 1900, and Manderston 'The Tea Room over the Dairy at Buxley' 1902.

LADYLAND DRAWINGS

NMRS Photographic Survey of designs for Ladyland, Ayrshire, including designs by David Hamilton 1816, 1821 and a survey of

Glengarnock Castle by Charles S S Johnston. *Copied 1965   (NMRS Inventory 2).*

K LAMM

Sketches of Scottish castles and houses by K Lamm 1862–1863 including: Cassilis; Castle Menzies; Faside; Kenmure House; Lochnaw Castle; Loch-an-Eilean; Rowallan; Scotstarvit Tower; Sorn Castle; and Winton House. *Presented by Ian Gow.*

LARGS, 'THE MOORINGS' DRAWINGS COLLECTION

A large collection of designs for 'The Moorings', Largs, by James Houston and others 1935–1973, including: designs for development of site by A Procuranti, Pistoia *c.*1929; designs by James Houston 1935; and

many designs for alterations, interior decorations, etc.
Presented by J B J Houston, 1989.

LASSWADE ESTATE

Sale Catalogue, 1888. Lindsay, Jamieson & Haldane, CA, 24 St Andrew Square, Edinburgh. With map and list of rentals.

HARRY BEDFORD LEMERE (1864–1944), Photographer

A large collection of negatives taken by Bedford Lemere of buildings and their interiors in Scotland including: The Hill House, Helensburgh by Charles Rennie Mackintosh; Craigcrook Castle; Gosford; Jenners, Princes Street, Edinburgh; Inglewood, Alloa; McEwan Hall, Edinburgh; Miss Cranston's Tea Room, 91 Buchanan Street, Glasgow; Alloa Public Baths; Hallyburton House; Mount Stuart; Finlaystone; Marischal College, Aberdeen; and the architect James Miller's house, Glasgow, etc. 1890–1928.
Presented per NMR (England).

GAVIN S A LENNOX, Architect

Miscellaneous papers including: school writing-book; family photographs including photograph of Gavin Lennox's wedding; sketchbook, Insc.: 'G S A Lennox, The Bield, Chryston' with views of buildings and scenery in Perthshire and Argyllshire; draft and typescript of a thesis on Crossraguel Abbey, illustrated with sketches, submitted to University of Glasgow for B.Sc. in Architecture; sketches of Melrose Abbey in a folder Insc.: 'The Lorimer Memorial Prize 1937–1938' with motto 'Bella'; a sketch of Dunblane Cathedral; a design for a bungalow by Lennox and MacMath, 103 Bath Street, Glasgow (his own house?—appears in photograph album); printed 'Guiding Instructions' by the Regent Oil Company for the design of garages and filling stations issued to 'Lennox and MacMath, FRIBA, Regional Architect, Glasgow Division 1935'; *Versailles and the Trianons*, no date; Advertising

Brochure for *Leoch* Stone Quarries Dundee, illustrated with photographs of Quarries and buildings constructed with Leoch stone; Lawrence Weaver, *The Scottish National War Memorial*, Country Life, 1927.

DAVID LIND. Portrait

DAVID LIND (1797–1856), Builder

Portrait. Photogravure after a pen sketch.

Lithograph of Scott Monument by James Somerville after G M Kemp 15 August 1840, Insc.: 'David Lind Esq.', issued as a receipt to subscribers to auxiliary fund for elevating structure to full extent. Said to come from Lind family's lawyer. Lind was the builder of the Scott Monument.
Purchased.

IAN G LINDSAY (1906–1966), Architect

Thirty-one sketch books, many bearing his

IAN G LINDSAY. Decorative covers of his notebooks

crest of a bird holding a key in its beak and dated from 1923–1935, covering a diverse range of architectural and antiquarian subjects, including: Scottish architecture, with many early sketches of tower houses; English architecture and parish churches; Italy; Norway; sketches of galleys illustrated on West Highland stones at Iona and Warrior's dress, etc; sketch surveys of existing buildings and notes relating to jobs, etc.

A file of research material on Scottish Churches.

A file of research material on Scottish Doocots.

Three sketch designs for houses in a Scottish style 'April 1922'.

Typescript lists with maps of 'Little Houses' in Scottish towns, compiled by I G Lindsay during the late 1930s; files include many photographs.
Presented by Mrs Christine McWilliam as part of the McWilliam Collection, 1989.

Contract of Partnership between Ian G Lindsay, George Hay and John Reid, 1959.

Two 'Twinlock' binders of Job Numbers for commissions numbered W/1 Iona Abbey— W/662 Polwarth Terrace, recording drawings issued, draughtsmen who executed them, dates sent, etc., with a loose typed alphabetical index, 1939–1967.

The Office Drawings of Ian G Lindsay and Partners; a very large collection including: King's College Chapel, Aberdeen; Aldie Castle; Ayr Old Kirk; Bathgate Episcopal Church; Castle Stalker; Corrour; Culross; Culzean Castle; Dunkeld; Edinburgh University; Glasgow Cathedral; St Mary's Haddington; Houston House; Inveraray Castle and Town; Iona Abbey; Lennoxlove; Makerstoun; Murthly Castle; Newbattle Abbey; Paisley Abbey; Preston Tower; Rossdhu House; Wemyss Castle, etc. *Deposited by John Reid, 1973 (NMRS Inventory 144).*

Photograph files of works executed by this firm.

Twenty-six notebooks and sketchbooks from 1923 with sketch designs, record surveys and site notes and a Cash Book January 1952–April 1964.

A folder of certificates for design awards from Civic Trust, Saltire Society, etc. 1959–1980. *Deposited by John Reid, 1983.*

MS Lists of Historic Buildings in Scotland, with associated maps of Scottish Burghs, marking locations 1936–1938.

LINPLUM HOUSE ALBUM

Photograph album with a survey of Linplum House (East Lothian), interiors and gardens, *c*.1910.

ALFRED G LOCHEAD (*c*.1888–1972), Architect

A collection of architectural papers including: an album, Insc.: 'Scrapbook of Architecture' containing four sketches of Gothic ornament and early photographs *c*.1860; four sketchbooks 1920–1922 with survey sketches and details of English parish churches, Wells Cathedral, Glasgow Cathedral, Paisley Abbey, and Balmanno Castle, including furniture; a scrapbook (possibly made up to Lorimer's specification), containing cuttings of works by him and buildings in Scandinavia; and a large collection of negatives and photographs of buildings designed by Lochead and a file of

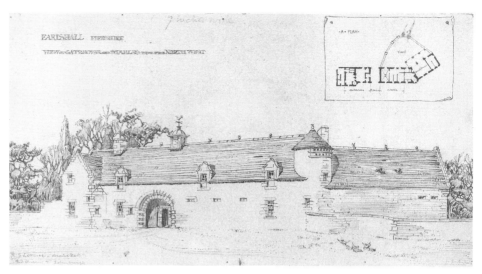

SIR ROBERT LORIMER. Design for Earlshall Gatehouse

cuttings and photographs, Insc.: 'Staircases'. *Deposited by Dr David M Walker, 1988.*

LOCHNAW DRAWINGS

NMRS Photographic Survey of drawings for Lochnaw Castle including: portfolio of designs by James Gillespie Graham (after 1816); portfolio of designs for castellated additions attributed to Archibald Elliot, no date; working drawings for Elliot's additions; designs for the Library at Edmond Castle, Cumberland, by Sir Robert Smirke, and surveys and designs for Leswalt Church. *Copied 1987 (NMRS Inventory 163)*

LOCKHART OF LEE DRAWINGS

NMRS Photographic Survey of the Lockhart of Lee Drawings including: many designs for farm and estate buildings, some by Peter Hamilton 1850s; and designs for Carnwath Gasworks by James Leslie 1857. *Copied 1971 (NMRS Inventory 29).*

SIR ROBERT LORIMER (1864–1929), Architect

The Office Drawings. A very large collection comprising: preliminary sketches, surveys, working drawings, related designs by craftsmen for furniture, stained glass, etc., exhibition drawings and some manuscript material covering almost all of the buildings designed by Sir Robert Lorimer and the firm's subsequent partnerships. A few private commissions for members of his family, etc., appear to be missing. The drawings include: Earlshall, his first important work 1892; the Colinton Cottages, Edinburgh from 1893; Brakenburgh and Rowallan 1901; Marly Knowe 1902; Barton Hartshorn 1902; Ardkinglas 1906; Lympne Castle 1907; Rhuna-Haven 1907; The Thistle Chapel, St Giles, Edinburgh 1909; Dunderave Castle 1911; Marchmont 1914; Dunrobin Castle 1915; Balmanno 1916; The Scottish National War Memorial, Edinburgh Castle 1919; Stowe Chapel 1927, etc. The collection also comprises a very large group of designs for War Memorials, both public (including many designs for the Imperial War Graves Commission) and private. Many of the drawings are published in Peter Savage, *Lorimer and the Edinburgh Craft Designers,*

SIR ROBERT LORIMER. Vault of the Thistle Chapel

1980. Although most were deposited by Sir Robert and Stuart Matthew in 1960, there have been a number of subsequent purchases of individual groups of drawings, specifications, etc. It was a condition of the deposition that the collection should be housed separately from the rest of the Record Collection, and this arrangement has been maintained. The collection is arranged alphabetically by title. Through the kind assistance of Dr Savage a number of stray rolls were reunited with the main body of the collection in 1988.

A collection of specifications including: Ardkinglas; Ashley House, Ratho; Belhaven House, Dunbar; Brakenbrough; Briglands; Coulston; Mr Craig's House, North Berwick; Dawyck House, Stobo; Edinburgh: House at Craiglockhart; The Scottish National War Memorial; University of Edinburgh Zoology Building; Cottage for Miss Guthrie Wright; Glasgow, St Mark's Episcopal Church; The Grange, North Berwick; Hyndford, North Berwick; Cottage, Linlithgow Bridge; Macedonian Military Cemeteries; Marchmont House; Monzie Castle; Paisley Abbey; Pitkerro; and Shirvan, Lochgilphead.

A box of miscellaneous correspondence, estimates, etc. discovered inside rolls of drawings during cataloguing.

A collection of papers relating to Sir Robert Lorimer's work for James Morton of Morton Sundour Fabrics, Carlisle, including: drawings and correspondence relating to new Factory buildings at Carlisle; Tuethur House for James Morton; alterations to Craigie Hall House, Edinburgh; and correspondence with firms supplying furnishings and fittings, including Messrs Whytock and Reid and Scott Morton Ltd *c*.1915–1930.
Presented by J W Morton, Carlisle, 1971.

Specification for St Andrew's University Library 1907.
Presented by Robert Hurd and Partners.

Index to Lorimer Office Correspondence deposited in Edinburgh University Library and miscellaneous contemporary photographs, etc., collected by Dr Peter Savage during his researches on this architect.
Presented by Dr Peter Savage, 1989.

SIR ROBERT LORIMER. Model for the Scottish National War Memorial

Model in painted wood and plaster for the Scottish National War Memorial *c*.1924.

A collection of progress photographs of the Scottish National War Memorial 1920s.

SIR ROBERT LORIMER, Architect and PERCY PORTSMOUTH, Sculptor

Plaster Maquette for Naval War Memorials at Chatham, Plymouth and Portsmouth.

LORIMER: MARGARET SWAN'S SCOTTISH NATIONAL WAR MEMORIAL ALBUM. Sample letterhead from album

SIR ROBERT LORIMER: MARGARET SWAN'S SCOTTISH NATIONAL WAR MEMORIAL ALBUM

An album of photographs and press cuttings compiled by Sir Robert Lorimer's Secretary, Margaret S Swan (née Margaret Brown), containing a wide variety of material including sketches, photographs and press-cuttings pertaining to the design and execution of the Scottish National War Memorial 1919–1962.
Presented by Mrs Margaret Swan per Rev. Mr Fergus Harris.

THE LOTHIAN COAL COMPANY

Catalogue of 'Bricks and every description of Fire Clay Goods' Whitehill and Polton Collieries, Brick and Fire Clay Works Rosewell, Midlothian. No date *c*.1910 Illustrated with lithographs.

VIEWS IN THE LOTHIANS

Album entitled 'Views in the Lothians' containing a large collection of engravings,

THE LOTHIAN COAL COMPANY.
Catalogue, title page

etchings, photographs of castles, country houses and towns in the Lothians c.1730–1890. Includes some rare ephemeral views and an etching of 'Woodburn, near Dalkeith' by H W Williams. Compiled by the Hon. Sir Hew Hamilton-Dalrymple c.1920.
Purchased at the sale of his Library in 1945 for £2.00.

LOUR HOUSE DRAWINGS

NMRS Photographic Survey of drawings for Lour House, including designs for additions of pavilions by Reginald Fairlie 1928.
Copied 1979   (NMRS Inventory 110).

LOW FARTHINGBANK, Dumfriesshire

NMRS Photographic Survey of plans for Low Farthingbank, including designs by either Charles Howitt or David Stitt, both Clerks of Works to the Dukes of Buccleuch 1865–1873.
Copied 1974   (NMRS Inventory 65).

A W LYONS

A collection of record drawings of Scottish painted ceilings by A W Lyons, many undertaken in connection with his published articles in the *Proceedings of the Society of Antiquaries of Scotland* 1896–1897, including: Pinkie House; Stobhall Castle; Aberdour Castle; Earlshall; Nunraw; St Mary's,

Grandtully; Balbegno Castle; Huntingtower Castle; Aberdour Castle; Cessnock Castle; Old Largs Church; Grange House; Bo'ness; Turriff Church; Falkland Palace; Palace of Mary of Guise, Lawnmarket, Edinburgh.
Society of Antiquaries of Scotland MSS 475   (NMRS Inventory 133).

LESLIE GRAHAME MACDOUGALL.
Design for St Andrew's Square, Edinburgh

LESLIE GRAHAME MACDOUGALL (1896–1974), Architect

The Office Drawings including: designs for the Reid Memorial Church, Edinburgh, 1929–1933; The National Bank of Scotland, St Andrew Square, Edinburgh, 1936; the Caledonian Insurance Company, Edinburgh, 1938; designs for the Hydro Electric Board, 1950s; and many buildings in the Oban area. The collection includes many exhibition drawings and competition entries.

(The architect was born Leslie Grahame Thomson).
Presented by Madame MacDougall, 1983.

Album of press-cuttings showing houses, churches, interiors, furniture, etc., admired by this architect, many from *Country Life*.
Purchased at sale of his library, 1983.

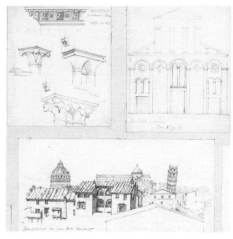

DAVID MACGIBBON. Detail from his Italian sketchbook

DAVID MACGIBBON (1831–1902), Architect

(RIAS) Photograph album with large size photographs of the outstanding Roman antiquities in Italy (e.g. Temple of Vesta at Tivoli); Gothic architecture in France and some Russian architectural subjects; each print Insc.: 'D MacGibbon' c.1870.

Fifteen sketchbooks 1855–1896 by David MacGibbon, A L MacGibbon and possibly Dr Thomas Ross, including: the Loire Chateaux, France 1855; Perthshire, including Dunblane, 1882; a trip to the west of Scotland and Iona 1892, and six sketchbooks (partially disbound) recording a trip to the Continent (France and Belgium) 1896.
Society of Antiquaries of Scotland MSS 463.

(RIAS) A collection of sketches, preparatory and finished drawings for the plates in *The Architecture of Provence and the Riviera*, 1888.

The Architecture of Provence and the Riviera, 1888. Proof copy (possibly ex-Edinburgh Architectural Association Library).

CHARLES MCGRORY PHOTOGRAPH COLLECTION

NMRS Survey of the Charles McGrory Collection of negatives in Campbeltown Public Library.
Surveyed 1981   (NMRS Inventory 139).

MACKENZIE AND MONCUR LTD

Catalogue of Horticultural Buildings, General Estate Buildings, Pavilions, etc., 1907. Registered Office and Works: Balcarres Street, Edinburgh. Illustrated with plans and photographs of workshops and with plans and photographs of conservatories erected throughout the British Isles, including the Royal Gardens at Windsor.

Advertising Brochure with catalogue and illustrations of buildings electrified by Mackenzie and Moncur c.1910.
Deposited by Mr A Mackenzie, 1981.

DR MACKAY MACKENZIE

A collection of lantern slides belonging to Dr Mackay Mackenzie, Secretary and Commissioner RCAHMS, relating to his Rhind Lectures on the medieval castle in Scotland, 1927.
Presented by the Rev. Robert Galloway, 1986.

ANDREW McKERRAL

Seventy-seven notebooks dealing with a very wide range of historical and antiquarian subjects 1938–1950s.
Presented by John Grant, 1976.

MACLAREN, SOUTER AND SALMOND, Architects

The office drawings of Maclaren, Souter and Salmond 1901–1925 including: Bellfield Street School, Dundee, 1915; additions to Benholm, 1926; 'Longcroft', Panmure Terrace, Dundee; Redmyre, Blackness Road, Dundee; alterations to Blairgowrie House, 1928; Medical Schools, University College, Dundee, 1902, etc.

MARY MACPHERSON

Sketchbook of Mary Macpherson 1899, including views of: Burleigh Bridge, Milnathort; Castle Campbell; Ochil View Road; Burleigh Castle; farms, etc. near Milnathort; The Salmon Fisher's Cottage, Leven, etc.

COLIN McWILLIAM. Drawing of the Surgeons' Hall, Edinburgh

COLIN McWILLIAM (1928–1989), Architect

A very large collection of slides relating to the Conservation course taught by Colin McWilliam at Edinburgh College of Art, but also bearing on his wide interests (the foreign slides transferred to the Department of Architecture, University of Edinburgh 1990); a collection of photographs relating to Colin McWilliam, *The Scottish Townscape*, 1975; a large collection of architectural postcards and

pamphlets, guidebooks, etc., collected during research for *The Buildings of Scotland: Lothian* 1978. See also under: The Rev. A L Drummond and I G Lindsay: Little Houses. *Presented by Mrs Christine McWilliam, 1989.*

A & J MAIN & CO

Illustrated Catalogue of Iron and Wire Fences, Hurdles, Gates, Railings, Etc. No date. c.1880 54 Gordon Street, Glasgow.

MANDERSTON DRAWINGS

NMRS Photographic Survey of drawings for Manderston House including: designs by John Kinross 1901; designs for cottages and estate buildings; 19th-century designs for Hamilton House, Newmarket by G Trollope and Sons; designs for a house by A Gilkie 1789; drawings of a design for Manderston by John White 1784; plans for Greenhouses at Manderston by Mackenzie and Moncur 1894; and copies of associated documents and contracts.
Copied 1983   (NMRS Inventory 156).

LUDOVIC McL MANN. Mann at Knappers Quarry, Dunbarton

LUDOVIC McL MANN (d.1955)

An extensive collection of newspaper cuttings, sketch plans and glass slides, copied for the NMRS, exhibit the interest generated by L McL Mann's excavations at Knappers burial

47

site 1937–9, and his astronomical interpretation of the site.

MAPS

Central to the Archaeological Collections are the Record Maps at 1:10,000 and 1:10,560 scale of the former Archaeology Branch of the Ordnance Survey, and these are constantly updated. The collection also includes a complete set of annotated OS '6-inch' 1st edition maps (1845–78), which were transferred from the National Museum of Antiquities of Scotland, and an annotated OS '6-inch' 2nd edition (1898–1940), part of the RCAHMS fieldwork collection.

THOMAS PURVES MARWICK (1854–1927) and THOMAS WALLER MARWICK (c.1901–1971), Architects

The Office Drawings including designs by T P Marwick for the Merchant Company Offices, Hanover Street, Edinburgh 1901 and designs for the Headquarters of St Cuthbert's Cooperative Association, Bread Street, Edinburgh, 1898, etc. The T W Marwick drawings include designs for his St Cuthbert's Cooperative Association Showrooms, Bread Street, Edinburgh, in 1937, and designs for pavilions in the Glasgow Empire Exhibition 1938, including the Atlantic Restaurant, etc.
Presented by T W Marwick, 1969.

MASONS' MARKS

A collection of sketches of masons' marks throughout Scotland (e.g. Arbroath Abbey, Elgin Cathedral, Mar's Wark, Stirling) 1861.
Society of Antiquaries of Scotland MSS 94.

J HARRISON MAXWELL (d.1971)

Collection of photographs and drawings, plans and notes of Maxwell's excavations of Ferniegair burials and cists 1936; Keil Cave 1933–4; Cultoquhey chambered cairn 1957; and Monzie standing stone (Witches Stone) 1958.

J HARRISON MAXWELL. Crannog excavation at Dumbuck, Dunbarton

Collection of slides illustrating the excavation of a crannog at Dumbuck in the Clyde estuary 1898, from sketches (some of a satirical character) by the excavator, Mr Donnelly.

SIR FRANK C MEARS (1880–1953), Architect

A collection of glass lantern slides used in town-planning lectures, including Scottish subjects (e.g. Stirling, Greater Dublin Reconstruction, Austria, Palestine, etc.).

EDWARD MELDRUM (d.1989), Architect

A collection of measured drawings and designs for additions and alterations to buildings in Inverness and North East Scotland including: measured drawings of Arbuthnot Church by Edward Meldrum undertaken while he was a student at Aberdeen School of Architecture 1947–1948; measured drawings by Edward Meldrum of Glenbuchat Kirk and Provost Skene's House, Aberdeen; designs for Castle Stuart, Erchless Castle, Leys Castle, Inches House, Inverness Steam Laundry, etc. c.1900–1950.
Presented by Edward Meldrum, 1987.

MELLERSTAIN DRAWINGS

NMRS Photographic Survey of drawings for Mellerstain including: designs attributed to William Adam 1725; design for a 'Ruinous Building to be placed on top of the Hill' by Robert Adam 1770s; a collection of mid 18th-century alternative designs for a new house; designs for Mellerstain House by Robert Adam 1770–1778; designs for a Palace copied from Sir Edward Lovett Pearce's design for a Lodge at Richmond for George II; mid 18th-century copies of Roger Morris's designs for Inveraray Castle; plan of the Canal by William Adam; designs for Coldstream Bridge, and coloured record drawings of original ceiling colours before repainting by J G Lindsay, Galashiels, 1898.
Copied 1978   (NMRS Inventory 94).

MELROSE ABBEY. Photograph collection

MELROSE ABBEY

A large collection of photographs of Melrose Abbey c.1865, possibly taken by William Donaldson Clerk.

MILLEARNE DRAWINGS

NMRS survey of papers at Millearne including: receipts from David MacGibbon & Son 1826; John Fraser, Painter, Perth; William Cooper, Glazier; Mr Hunt, Ironside Place, decorated glass; Harris Watson, ornamental stoves, 16 Oxford Street; Chamberlain and Co., Worcester Royal Porcelain works *re* encaustic tiles 1843; and a lithograph of the Library at Millearne by J & W Smith, Edinburgh.
Surveyed 1968   (NMRS Inventory 9).

JAMES MILLER (1860–1947), Architect

(RIAS) The surviving Office Drawings including: Belmont Church 1892; Glasgow University, Natural Philosophy Building 1904; Glasgow Royal Infirmary 1906; Newark Castle 1907; Kildonan House 1916; The Royal Scottish Automobile Club, Glasgow 1923; Warehouse Building, Renfrew Street, Glasgow 1928; Messrs Coats Administration Building 1931; The Institute of Civil Engineers, Great George Street, London 1935; Empire Exhibition Glasgow 1938; The Gosford Furnishing Co. Ltd, Cotton Street, Glasgow 1950. (Includes many drawings by James Miller and Son and Manson).

THE PETER MILLER COLLECTION

(RIAS) A large collection of drawings collected (and possibly salvaged) by Peter Miller, who was apprenticed to Scott Morton and Co. and was subsequently employed as a designer in its drawing office; after the firm went into liquidation in 1966, he became chief designer with Messrs Whytock and Reid (who had purchased the goodwill). The earliest item in the collection is a catalogue of *c*.1770 for composition enrichments for chimney-pieces. Scott Morton's design archive is also represented by many pages from his 'Scrapbook', consisting of cuttings and engraved designs derived from a very wide variety of sources. Two portfolios of design drawings include a design for a London drawing room of *c*.1880, designs for 'Redlands', Great Western Road, Glasgow *c*.1895, and many designs executed by Scott Morton and Co. for works in association with

THE PETER MILLER COLLECTION.
Design for a four-post bedstead by Whytock and Reid

Sir Robert Lorimer. The collection also holds finished drawings and sketches by John Kinross for his *Details of Italian Buildings*, 1882, which were possibly presented to David Ramsay, Chief Designer of Scott Morton and Co. A superb set of pencil survey drawings of furniture was possibly subsequently also inherited from Ramsay by Peter Miller. The collection also includes a very large collection of photograph albums and loose photographs of works executed by Scott Morton and Co. from 1890–1966 arranged by type (e.g. 'Church pews', 'Communion tables', 'Bank Interiors', etc.). The manuscript material includes: a draft of Peter Miller's autobiography covering his earliest days with Scott Morton and Co.; the 'Job Number Book' which includes a chronological list of all the designers who worked in the Scott Morton Drawing Office from the 1890s, with comments on their character and abilities; and a complete list of works by Scott Morton and Co. Peter Miller's own designs included many iconographical schemes for Catholic Churches. The collection also embraces a number of plaster casts of modelled ornaments, etc. A

series of folders containing designs for 'tables', 'beds', etc., is undoubtedly by Whytock and Reid and dates from 1900–1940.

MILLPORT, CUMBRAE, THE CATHEDRAL OF THE ISLES

NMRS Photographic Survey of drawings for the Cathedral of the Isles including designs by William Butterfield 1849–50 and record drawings of Iona Abbey by J C and C A Buckler.
Copied 1979   (NMRS Inventory 103).

J DONALD MILLS (1872–1958) AND GODFREY SHEPHERD (1874–1937), Architects

The Office Drawings including: alterations to Megginch Castle 1928; restoration of Fingask Castle 1925; 9 Abbotsford Crescent, St Andrews 1904; Abergeldie Mains and alterations to buildings on Balmoral Estates 1923–1924; The White House, Hepburn Gardens, St Andrews 1904; alterations to Ardblair House 1955; and a design for Abernethy War Memorial 1920.

MINTO HOUSE

Portfolio. A very large bound volume, Insc.: "Working Drawings of Minto House The Seat of the Rt. Honble. The Earl of Minto'. (Archibald Elliot *c*.1814).

MINTON, HOLLINS AND CO.

Catalogue. 1867. With coloured lithographs showing encaustic tessellated pavements and including a price list.

MINTON, HOLLINS AND CO. Catalogue design for pavement of tessellated tiles

MONYMUSK DRAWINGS

NMRS Photographic Survey of drawings for Monymusk including: plan for improvements to the Policy by Robert Robinson; designs for an addition by William Burn 1838; and copies of associated documents.
Copied 1972   (NMRS Inventory 45).

MORAY ESTATE DRAWINGS

NMRS Photographic Survey of the Moray Estate drawings including designs for housing, farm buildings, etc., throughout the Moray Estates 1871–1913, and related extracts from Factor's Account Books.
Copied 1971   (NMRS Inventory 32).

MORRIS SINGER COMPANY

Advertising Brochure. *Architectural Metalwork* (Branch of William Morris and Co. (Westminster), Dorset Road, London SW8) *c.*1935, with photographic illustrations of work in England, and a British Linen Bank by Walter Todd, Architect, in Edinburgh.

A H MOTTRAM (1886–1953), Architect

Three sketchbooks.
1 Insc.: (on cover) 'A H Mottram Sketches 1907 April to August 1907 Norwich, Porthleven, Hampstead Garden City, Letchworth' including: Portrait of 'Mrs Marshall, Technical School April 22 1907'; armour; anatomy; St John Sepulchre, Norwich; Porthleven, Ship Inn; ducks and rabbits; portraits of Green, Waterhouse, Mr L'Etranger; Wyldwood Farm; Wyldes, etc.
2 Insc.: (on cover) 'Sketch Book Rosyth, Kirk Newton, Peterboro' 111 George Street, Edinburgh' including: notes on 60 houses at Rosyth 1922; sketch surveys; Crossroads Place School, Rosyth; Kinghorn; Oban; Islay 1948; Urquhart Castle, Loch Ness; Bellandoch Hotel, Crinan Canal; Duart Castle; Iona, Main Street, etc.
3 Insc.: 'A H Mottram ARIBA Maryville, Gullane 29 VIII (19)30' including: doorway in Canongate, Jedburgh; Kelso; Alnwick; Yetholm; The Plough, Yetholm; Weston

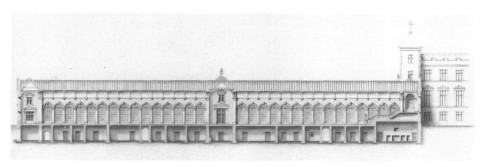

MURTHLY CASTLE DRAWINGS. Design for a conservatory by James Gillespie Graham

Church near Bristol 1931; Clapton Church; Cheddar; Wells; notes on Bristol and Wales; sketches of houses in Bristol; Grantown-on-Spey 1931; Kingussie; Inverness Town House; Chimney; King's House, Glencoe; Cannich 1932; All Saints Church, Norwich 1935; Cawston Church 1935; Happisburgh Church; Binham 1938, etc.
Presented by Ian Gow.

MOUNTQUHANIE HOUSE DRAWINGS

NMRS Photographic Survey of drawings at Mountquhanie including designs of 1804 and a design for additions by James Craig 1770.
Copied 1969   (NMRS Inventory 21).

MOUNT STUART HOUSE

Sale Catalogue. John Baxter, 243 St Vincent Street, Glasgow, December 1920. 'Conditional to its complete demolition and removal by the Purchaser. Suitable for re-erection as a Hotel-Hydro, Restaurant, Casino, Public Buildings, Etc'.
Illustrated with photographs.

MOXON AND CARFRAE, House-painters and Decorators

Three note books with measurements of executed paintwork covering 1815, 1816, 1820,

1821, 1828, 1831 and 1832, including: work at Dalmeny Church; Brancepeth Castle, Northumberland; Whittinghame; Perth County Buildings; Alderston; Dumfries House; and many houses in the New Town of Edinburgh. (N.B. Probably compiled by one of Moxon and Carfrae's predecessors who subsequently amalgamated with the firm).

MURTHLY CASTLE DRAWINGS

(RIAS) Portfolio, Insc.: 'Plans of the Proposed Addition to Murthly Castle by James Gillespie, Edinburgh 1822' with plans and sections of Saloon.

(RIAS) Portfolio, Insc.: 'Design of the Conservatory Proposed for Murthly by James Gillespie Graham Edinr. 1840' with elevations, plans and sections of the conservatory.

(RIAS) A small collection of drawings relating to Murthly and Estate, including a floor plan of the new Murthly Castle, a section of a Library in the old Castle, and a floor plan of a hospital on flimsy *c.*1840.

MURTHLY CHAPEL

Portfolio. 'Design for the Proposed Chapel at Murthly by James Gillespie Graham Edinburgh 20th December 1841.' Elevations, plan, sections and perspective view looking to altar. Similar to, but simpler than executed scheme.
Presented by Inverness Museum.

The Chapel of St Anthony the Eremite at Murthly Perthshire The Seat of Sir William Drummond Stewart of Grandtully Bart. Lithographed by Schenk and Ghemar from the Designs of James Gillespie Graham and Alexander Christie, ARSA, Edinburgh, 1850.

MURTHLY CHAPEL. Design by James Gillespie Graham

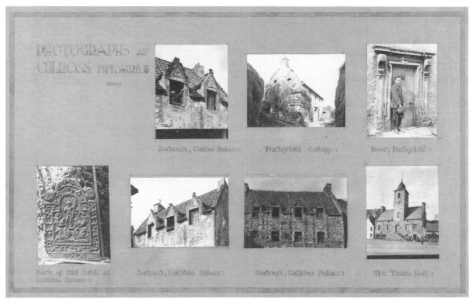

MUTUAL HOUSEHOLDS ASSOCIATION FOR SCOTLAND

Correspondence, plans, reports, minutes, etc. and a membership leaflet illustrated by David M Walker, 1971–1981. The object of the Association was to preserve Scottish country houses.
Presented by C H Cruft.

THE NATIONAL ART SURVEY OF SCOTLAND

1,500 sheets of measured survey drawings of palaces, churches, castles, decorative detail, plasterwork and furniture, etc., prepared by the National Art Survey Bursars at the Edinburgh School of Applied Art (founded

THE NATIONAL ART SURVEY OF SCOTLAND. Exhibition panel showing Culross and survey of a ceiling at Holyrood

1892) under the personal supervision of the Director, Sir Rowand Anderson. From 1895, the Bursars, selected from the best draughtsmen trained by the school, were appointed each year. The surveys were undertaken during the summer and the finished pencil and colour wash drawings were prepared during the winter. The completed drawings were preserved in the school to create a library of exemplars which Anderson intended should imbue the students with a traditional Scottish idiom of design. In 1903 Anderson's school was amalgamated with the Board of Manufacturers' School of Art to found Edinburgh College of Art, but the bursaries were continued. Although attempts were made to involve the other Scottish art schools, only Glasgow played an active part. From 1907 the original drawings were preserved by the newly established Trustees of the National Gallery of Scotland, but Anderson pressed for a set of tracings to be made for the Edinburgh College's use. Anderson's concern for the NASS led to pressure from the newly founded Institute of

Scottish Architects which resulted in publication of the drawings. *The National Art Survey of Scotland, Examples of Scottish Architecture from the 12th to the 17th Century* appeared in four volumes between 1921 and 1933. In 1958 the Trustees of the National Galleries presented the original drawings to the Royal Commission on the Ancient and Historical Monuments of Scotland, and the tracings were presented to the Scottish National Buildings Record. In 1966 the sets were amalgamated on the foundation of the National Monuments Record of Scotland. The drawings cover a very wide range of building types from Linlithgow Palace, Holyrood and the Border Abbeys to 18th-century Country Houses like Pollok and Dumfries House. The collection includes tower houses and many urban buildings in Stirling and Edinburgh. See I Gow, 'Sir Rowand Anderson's National Art Survey of Scotland', *Architectural History*, Vol 27, 1984 pp. 543–554.

Photographs. They seem to have been taken primarily for exhibition panels displayed alongside the finished survey drawings in the annual exhibitions of the work of the Edinburgh School of Applied Art. Twenty-five exhibition panels survive, and a few show the Bursars engaged in survey work.
Presented by the Trustees of the National Galleries of Scotland, 1958.

THE NATIONAL TRUST FOR SCOTLAND QUINQUENNIAL SURVEYS OF PROPERTIES

Quinquennial survey reports prepared on the properties of the National Trust for Scotland, architects' reports, plans and photographs 1987–88.
Deposited by the National Trust for Scotland.

DAVID NEAVE (1773–1841), Architect

(RIAS) A volume of record drawings of designs executed in Dundee and district. (c. 160 designs) including: a very wide range of villas, many 'recently building'; profiles, joinery details, funerary monuments, etc., 1815–1819; and designs for Tay Street, Dundee.

NOAD (b.1906) AND WALLACE, Architects

(RIAS) Photograph Album. Illustrating 'The Estate of Broadmeadows, Symington, Ayrshire, started 1931 finished 1934'. 'Noad and Wallace's first job'.

NORTH OF SCOTLAND ARCHAEOLOGICAL SERVICES (NOSAS)

Founded by John Hedges in 1976–7, with funding from HBM/SDD, NOSAS was created to undertake long-term rescue excavations, to promote archaeological fieldwork and research, and to deal with any archaeological emergency in the north of Scotland, Orkney and Shetland. The collection comprises excavation and publication drawings, photographs and negatives, colour slides, notebooks, correspondence, registers and miscellaneous items from all NOSAS projects, including: Isbister chambered cairn; Liddle burnt mound; Tougs burnt mound; and Bu broch. NOSAS was disbanded in 1982.
Presented by J Hedges.

THE NORTHERN LIGHTHOUSE BOARD

A very large collection of designs for lighthouses administered by the Northern Lighthouse Board and including those designed by the Stevenson family. Including: Ailsa Craig; Ardnamurchan; Auskerry; Barns Ness; Barra Head; Bass Rock; Bell Rock; Bressay; Buchan Ness; Butt of Lewis; Cairnbulg; Calf of Man; Calvay; Cantick Head; Cape Wrath; Cava; Chanonry; Chicken Rock; Corran; Corsewell Point; Covesea Skerries; Cromarty; Davaar; Douglas Head; Dubh Artach; Duncansby Head; Dunnet Head; Dunollie; Eilean Glas; Esha Ness; Eyre Point, Raasay; Fair Isle North; Fair Isle South; Fidra; Fife Ness; Fladda; Flannan Isles; Girdle Ness; Helliar Holm; Hestan Island; Holburn Head; Holy Island; Hoy High; Hoy Low; Hysheir; Inchkeith; Isle of May; Isle of Oransay; Kerrera; Killantringan; Kinnaird Head; Kyleakin; Kylerhea; Lady Isle; Lady Rock; Langness; Lismore; Little Ross; Loch Eriboll; Lochindaal; Loch Ryan; Lother Rock; McArthurs Head; Maughold Head; Monarch Islands; Muckle Flugga; Mull of Galloway;

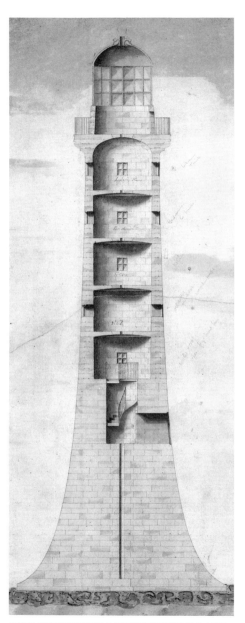

THE NORTHERN LIGHTHOUSE BOARD.
Cross section of Bell Rock Lighthouse

Mull of Kintyre; Neist Point; North Ronaldsay; Noss Head; Noup Head; Out Skerries; Oxcars; Pentland Skerries; Point of Ayre; Rattray Head; Rinns of Islay; Rona; Rubh Nan Gall; Rubh Re; Ruvaal; St Abbs; Sanda; Scurdie Ness; Skerryvore; Skerviulle; Start Point; Stoer Head; Stornoway; Stroma; Stromness; Sule Skerry; Sumburgh Head; Suther Ness; Tarbat Ness; Tiumpan Head; Tod Head;Turnberry; Ushenish.
Deposited by the Northern Lighthouse Board 1986.

NORTHERN LIGHTHOUSES ALBUM

Photograph album with a large collection of commercial and amateur photographs and engravings of Scottish lighthouses and lightships. c.1900.

WILLIAM NOTMAN, Architect

A very large collection of drawings by this architect, who was a pupil of Playfair, but also including many drawings associated with his father, John Notman, who acted as a Clerk of Works to the Duke of Atholl, and various Edinburgh architects, including George Angus. The John Notman drawings include designs for Blair Castle, Dunkeld Cathedral and Gothic gates to Dunkeld House c.1820, etc. The William Notman drawings include many designs from the office of William Henry Playfair during the 1830s and early 1840s, including a competition entry of a design for the Western Cemetery, Glasgow, bearing the motto 'Alberti'. Notman's independent designs include 'The Elms', Whitehouse Loan, Edinburgh 1858, and the Star Inn at Moffat 1860, etc.
Presented by Mr and Mrs Notman, 1980.

Sketchbook, bearing label of 'R Ackermann's Repository of Arts, 101 Strand, London' (Paper watermarked 1822). Including: sketches of Arthur Lodge and Dean Orphanage, Edinburgh; surveys of monuments in Greyfriars Churchyard; ceilings in Lawnmarket, Queen Mary's Room, Holyrood, Moray House, Mitchell's Land, Cowgate, Roman Eagle Lodge, etc. (all in Edinburgh);

WILLIAM NOTMAN. The entrance to Dunkeld House by Archibald Elliot

and an unfinished sketch of Minto Manse.
Presented by Mr & Mrs Notman, 1981

Manuscripts. Miscellaneous papers associated with John Notman including: specification for a house for Alexander Goelen, Shipbuilder, Leith 1802; abstract of John Notman's claims on the Duke of Atholl 1818; specification of Abdie Church, no date; specification of Kirkcaldy Church, George Angus 1828. Papers relating to William Notman, pupil of William Henry Playfair including: specification of a house for Andrew Rutherfurd, St Colme Street 1825; specification for entrance Lodge, Lurgan 1834; specification for Barmore house 1836; specification for banking at Donaldson's Hospital 1840.

Papers relating to William Notman's architectural practice, including specifications for: Dalry, Bonded Warehouse 1855; Haymarket Distillery 1856; Shopfront 132 Princes Street 1857; McLean and Hope's Chemical Works, Leith 1860; Tenement, Fort Street, North Leith 1862; Brewery North Back of Canongate 1867; and Mr Hamilton's Villa at Greenhill.
Presented by Mr and Mrs Notman 1980.

T O'BRIEN SKETCHES

A collection of sketches of Picturesque Scottish buildings 1817–1823 including: Brechin; Dalkeith; Edinburgh (Calton Hill, Goldenacre Cottage, Leith Harbour and New Town Improvements); Glamis Castle; Lasswade; Melrose Abbey.
Presented by T O'Brien of SNPG, 1952.

ORDNANCE SURVEY ARCHAEOLOGY BRANCH

An extensive collection including 1:10,000 record sheets, 1:1250 and 1:2500 sheets and a set of 1st ed. '6–inch' maps; index cards; survey information; stereo vertical photographs taken by the RAF, as part of the 'National Survey' begun in 1946; a set of enlarged and rectified aerial photographs taken for the OS 1:2500 mapping survey; microfilm copies of the original County Name Books; library; correspondence and archive dating from the late 1940s to 1983. In 1983 this collection and the functions of the Scottish Archaeology Branch of the Ordnance Survey were transferred to the Royal Commission to help create a consolidated record of antiquities in Scotland.
Presented by the Ordnance Survey.

ORKNEY AND SHETLAND ISLANDS

An album of sketches of Orkney and Shetland by James Skene, August 1801, including views

of: Kirkwall; 'Brough of Culswick'; Lerwick, etc.
Society of Antiquaries of Scotland MSS 164.

OTTER HOUSE ALBUM

Photograph album with a view of Otter House, Argyllshire, and many unidentified architectural views.

OXENFORD CASTLE DRAWINGS

NMRS Photographic Survey of drawings for Oxenford Estate including: elevations drawn prior to 1780; design for offices; and a design for the bridge by Alexander Stevens 1783.
Copied 1972   (NMRS Inventory 41).

J D PARKER

Letters from J D Parker, Ashmolean Museum, to J T Irvine on various architectural subjects 1875–1883.
Society of Antiquaries of Scotland MSS 616.

A N PATERSON (1862–1947), Architect

Sketchbook. Insc: 'Alexander N Paterson July 1891'; and bearing four addresses 'Torwood, Row, Dumbartonshire', '2 St John's Terrace, Hillhead Glasgow', '136 Wellington Street, Glasgow' and 'The Long Croft, Helensburgh'. With sketches and measured surveys of architectural subjects in England and Scotland 1891, including: Kirby Hall, Oundle, Apethorpe Hall, Rushton Hall, Stamford, Bolsover, Haddon. Aberdeen including Victoria Lodging House (Provost Skene's House), Trades House, Drum Castle, Crathes, Craigievar, Midmar, Castle Frazer, Muchalls, Fyvie, Huntly, Elgin Cathedral, Fortrose Cathedral. In 1892 subjects include Kelso, Kellie Castle, St Andrews, Elie, Crail. The sketchbook was clearly taken up much later and includes also: a survey of Burnbrae, Helensburgh; a sketch of Maggie Paterson at her embroidery frame at The Long Croft, Helensburgh; and designs for colour decorations at Benvenue, Helensburgh.
Presented by Miss Viola Paterson, the Architect's daughter, per Ailsa Tanner, 1985.

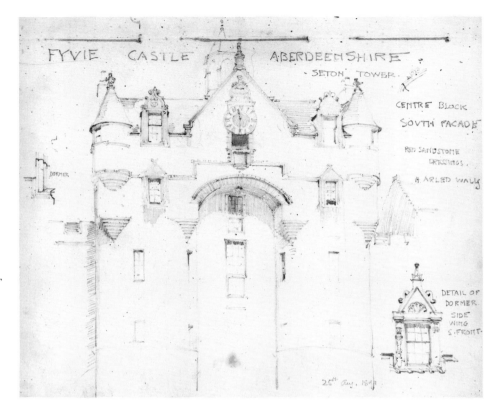

A N PATERSON. Sketch details, Fyvie Castle and group photograph at the Ecole des Beaux Arts, Paris

A collection of sketchbooks.
1 Insc: 'A N Paterson, 4 St John's Terrace, Glasgow' 1888–9 with sketches in Oxford and Italy including San Giovanni, Syracuse; Olympeium; Girgenti; Ravenna; Tivoli; Orvieto; Verona; Perugia; Prato; Bologna; Torcello; Brescia and a list of hotels and restaurants in Italy, with prices.
2 Insc: 'Alexander N Paterson, The Long Croft, Helensburgh' 1912–13 with sketches of Bamburgh, Loch Long, Kinloch Rannoch, the Chair of the Popes, Avignon, Arles, Rapallo, Boboli Gardens Florence, Morar, Loch Lomond, and Cumberland.
3 Insc: 'Alexander N Paterson, The Long Croft, Helensburgh, 1915' 1915–20. With

sketches of Scottish Scenery; Red Lion Hotel, Truro; the Farm, Zennor; Falmouth, etc.; Scottish scenery 1917; Surveys of National Bank of Scotland 1920; Port Office, Helensburgh; Woodend; 11 Kirklee Road; notes for Lenzie War Memorial; 60 Montgomerie Drive; Rowmore, Row: Garelochead; 22 Belhaven Terrace.

4 Sketches of a tour of Portugal including: Cintra, Villa Orotava, Icod, Santos Island, etc., February-April 1920.

5 Sketches of Portugal March 1920; Scottish scenery 1920; Italy 1922 including Assisi; Helensburgh Golf Course; The Long Croft, Helensburgh; and a design for a bookplate by Miss Paterson?

6 Insc: (on cover) '1934', 1931–1934. Including sketches of Italian Garden Inishcullen Island, Glengarriff Co. Cork; Bantry Bay; Irish scenery; Penshurst; Penshurst Place; The Leicester Arms Penshurst; Worthing; Viviers, Rhone; Vence; Carros; Tourette; Glencoe; Corpach; Strathnaver; Ullapool; Norfolk; Penshurst. With loose sheets from earlier sketchbooks including: Venice 1908; Franco-British Exhibition 1908; Klosterneuburg 1908; Lisbon 1920.

7 Insc: 'Alexander N Paterson, Helensburgh 1938', 1938–45. including sketches of Maiden Castle, Dorset; Dorchester; Chipping Camden; Stratford; Tunbridge Wells; Faslane; Iona; Kirkcudbright; a Hospital Ward, etc.
Purchased from Cyril Gerber Fine Art, Glasgow, 1985.

Designs for The Long Croft, Helensburgh (his own house), including working drawings 1902; designs for later alterations; garage, etc. 1930s.
Presented by Executors of Miss Viola Paterson, per Ailsa Tanner 1982.

A small collection of sketches of Scottish historic buildings drawn in 1888, but coloured and finished in 1943.

A N PATERSON PHOTOGRAPH COLLECTION

A collection of exhibition, publication and snapshot photographs illustrating buildings designed by A N Paterson, including: portraits of A N Paterson; Auchendennan Castle;

Glasgow Eye Infirmary, Charlotte Street; Muirend Branch of the Savings Bank of Glasgow; Temporary Exhibition Building at Kelvingrove Park; a design for the Royal Exchange; Gleddoch House; Gourock Municipal Buildings; The Long Croft, Helensburgh; Yarrow Kirk; Scalescleugh (Cumberland); and many war memorials throughout Scotland. Includes also a collection of snapshots showing the Paterson family at home at the Long Croft.
Presented by Miss Viola Paterson, 1985.

JOHN L PATERSON. Design for a chair

JOHN L PATERSON (d.1989), Architect

A large collection including: the Office Drawings; his portfolio; office correspondence; photographs; drawing instruments; research files for the Le Corbusier exhibition 1966 with typescripts of interviews with Le Corbusier's associates, etc; models; sketchbooks; presentation copies of catalogues for his exhibitions; two prototype chairs designed by Paterson; and a collection of exhibition panels.
Presented per Balfour and Manson.

WALLER HUGH PATON (1828–1895), Artist

Antiquarian sketches of standing stones, castles and churches including Old Alloway Kirk, Brodick, Castle Campbell, Claypotts,

WALLER HUGH PATON. Claypotts Castle

Craigmillar, Threave, Standing Stones of Stenness, etc. 1857–1882.
Presented by Mrs M Cross whose husband, Col. A R Cross, was a descendant of J N Paton.

NAN PATTULLO COLLECTION

A large collection of coloured slides of historic buildings and interiors throughout Scotland taken by Nan Pattullo for her lectures, a selection of which was published in her *Castles, Houses and Gardens in Scotland*, 1967, 1974.
Presented by Nan Pattullo, 1980 (NMRS Inventory 125).

ARTHUR BALFOUR PAUL (1875–1938), Architect

Photographic portrait c.1920.
Presented by W R Adams, 1982.

MISS PEARSON'S PHOTOGRAPH ALBUM

Photograph album compiled by Miss Pearson, daughter of Alexander Pearson of Luce Cottage, Annan, showing family and Salvesen houses in Scotland, including views of 'Miss Christie's Japanese Garden at Cowden Castle 1909.'

JOHN DICK PEDDIE (1824–1891) AND CHARLES G H KINNEAR (1830–1894), Architects

A small collection of designs by Peddie and Kinnear including: St Paul's Episcopal Church, Edinburgh 1891; Glen Gorm Castle, Mull (Sorne House) 1860; St Mary's Cathedral, Palmerston Place, Edinburgh 1873; Station Hotel, Princes Street, Edinburgh 1903; Scottish Equitable Life Assurance Co., 28 St Andrew Square, Edinburgh 1897; St John's Episcopal Church, Princes Street, Edinburgh 1879–1881; Royal Bank of Scotland, Bridgeton, Glasgow 1874; and sideboard for Taymouth Castle 1872, etc.

NMRS Index to the surviving Office Drawings of this long-established Edinburgh practice c.1858–1940, including many drawings by David Rhind, Sydney Mitchell, etc.; and with alphabetical index by address.
Listed 1978.

PENKAET CASTLE

Typescript history by A R Dufty, c.1955
Deposited by A R Dufty, 1989.

PERTH ALBUM

Photograph album with views of Perth neatly arranged within an accompanying historical text by an anonymous author, c.1890.

PERTH BUILDING SURVEY

Completed record sheets, survey sketches, photographs, and papers produced by the Perth Building Survey 1982–1983.
Deposited by Perth Building Survey per Jane Anderson.

PERTH COUNTY BUILDINGS DRAWINGS

NMRS Photographic Survey of drawings for County Buildings, Perth, including designs by Robert Reid 1806 and 1812–1814.
Copied 1974   (NMRS Inventory 59).

PERTH, HAL O' THE WYND'S HOUSE DRAWINGS

NMRS Photographic Survey of a collection of drawings discovered in Hal o' the Wynd's House 1980 and now in the Sandeman Library, Perth, including: contract drawings for Perth Poor's House c.1858 and designs for Public Wash House, Perth by David Corrie and Son c.1900.
Copied 1980   (NMRS Inventory 121).

PERTH, OLD ACADEMY BUILDING

A collection of designs for the Old Academy by Robert Reid 1803.
Deposited by Perth District Council.

PERTH, ST LEONARD'S IN THE FIELDS

A collection of designs and working drawings by J J Stevenson 1884.
Deposited by St Leonard's in the Fields, Perth, 1979.

PETERHEAD ALBUM

Photograph album with views of: Peterhead and vicinity; Old Deer; Aden House;

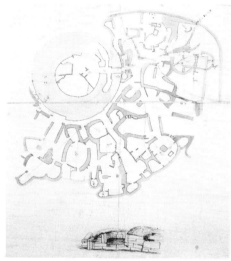

GEORGE PETRIE. Sketch and plan of Broch of Lingro, Orkney

Inverugie Castle; Ravenscraig; Slains Castle etc. c.1900.

GEORGE PETRIE (d.1875)

A collection of notebooks, sketchbooks and

correspondence relating to G Petrie's research on the history and archaeology of Orkney and Shetland, including his many excavations. G Petrie was Sheriff Clerk of Orkney and, from 1848, was a corresponding member of the Society of Antiquaries of Scotland, to whom his collection of papers was donated.
Society of Antiquaries of Scotland MSS 319, 332, 396, 423, 487.

STUART PIGGOTT (*b.* 1910)

While Abercromby Professor of Prehistoric Archaeology at Edinburgh University 1946–1975, Piggott carried out a series of excavations in Scotland. The collection includes: photographs and plans of Castle Law fort, Glencorse 1948–9; Cairnpapple Hill henge and cairns 1948; Torwoodlee broch 1950; Corrimony chambered cairn 1952; and Croft Moraig stone circle 1965.

PINKIEBURN ALBUM

Photograph album with a survey of Pinkieburn House, Musselburgh *c.*1900.

PITFIRRANE DRAWINGS

NMRS Photographic Survey of designs for Pitfirrane House and estate, including: design for proposed alterations *c.*1730; designs for additions 1811; designs for alterations by R Rowand Anderson (Wardrop and Anderson 1888); and many designs for estate and farm buildings.
National Library of Scotland MS 6509. Copied 1970 (NMRS Inventory 26).

JAMES PLAYFAIR (1755–1794), Architect

NMRS Photographic Survey of drawings by James Playfair in the Soane Museum including: Kippenross; Kinnaird Castle; Cairness; Cullen House and Town Hall; Anniston; Dalkeith House; Raith House; Dunninald; Murie House; Dupplin; Kirriemuir Church; Urie House; Langholm Lodge; Ardkinglas; and Baldovie House.
Copied 1975 (NMRS Inventory 55).

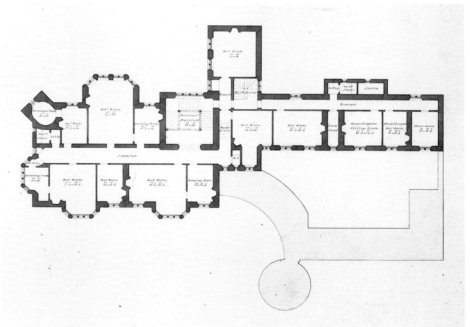

WILLIAM HENRY PLAYFAIR. Designs for Hillside House, Aberdour. Elevation and plan

WILLIAM HENRY PLAYFAIR (1790–1857), Architect

(RIAS) A collection of student drawings, presentation drawings, unfinished working drawings and sketches. The collection includes: studies after designs by William Burn, Thomas Hamilton, David Laing, Sir Robert Smirke, William Smirke and Benjamin Dean Wyatt, etc.; presentation drawings of preliminary designs including a perspective of

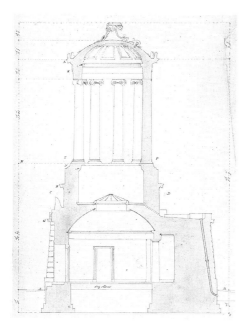

WILLIAM HENRY PLAYFAIR. Student drawing of Thomas Hamilton's design for Burns Monument

the Corinthian design for the Royal College of Surgeons, Edinburgh and the 'Roman villa' design for Brownlow House; unexecuted designs including Obelisk in memory of Sir Walter Scott and two designs for Hillside House, Aberdour; designs for previously unrecorded works including St Ronan's Well, Innerleithen; unfinished drawings relating to executed designs, including the Royal College of Surgeons, Edinburgh, the Edinburgh Observatory, Prestongrange, etc. and a sketch recording a site visit to Lauriston Castle, Edinburgh. This material must derive from the 'rump' of the Playfair collection not deemed worthy of preservation when Playfair's clerk, James A Hamilton, went through the office papers after Playfair's death and put together the complete sets of sequentially numbered working drawings for preservation in Edinburgh University Library.
Presented 'anonymously' to the Edinburgh Architectural Association.

A collection of designs for Edinburgh University, 1817 and Donaldson's Hospital 1842–1844.
Presented by R C Notman WS, 1968.

THE POST OFFICE

Photographs of Post Offices and Telephone Exchanges in Scotland 1950s–1970s.
Presented by the Property Services Agency, 1989.

POWELL AND SONS, Stained Glass Artists

A small collection of designs for stained glass for Scottish churches 1904–1915.

THOMAS PRINGLE (fl. 1890s), Engraver

(RIAS) A collection of student drawings, many executed while he attended the Edinburgh School of Applied Art during R Rowand Anderson's Directorship, 1894–6, and related material, including drawings submitted to South Kensington Examination Board, etc.
Presented by Mrs Sutherland.

RAEHILLS DRAWINGS

NMRS Photographic Survey of drawings at Raehills including; designs for additions to Raehills by William Burn 1829; a design for Raehills by Alexander Stevens c.1807; and many designs for estate buildings.
Copied 1980   (NMRS Inventory 115).

RAVELSTON HOUSE

Sale Catalogue. Illustrated, c.1915; Hope, Todd and Kirk WS, 19 Charlotte Square, Edinburgh.

REDNOCK HOUSE DRAWINGS

NMRS Photographic Survey of drawings for Rednock House including: designs by R Brown 1821; designs for the stables by James

Ramsay 1797; and designs for estate buildings.
Copied 1974   (NMRS Inventory 58).

RENFREWSHIRE AND BUTE

Postcard album containing a wide selection of subjects in Renfrewshire and Bute, compiled c.1939.

JAMES S RICHARDSON. Photograph album

JAMES S RICHARDSON, Principal Inspector of Ancient Monuments Scotland.

Six notebooks and a photograph album, containing research notes and drafts of articles. Subjects include Stirling Castle, an introduction to the Sculptured Monuments at Kilmory Knap, Argyll, and useful notes for an antiquarian visiting Paris. Illustrated with sketches and measured surveys. Photograph album contains records of sculptured stones in Argyll and group portrait of the 'Ancient Monument Research Party, Poltalloch, April 15th–18th 1928'.

SIR IAN A RICHMOND (1902–1965)

Responsible for the pioneering excavations of Roman forts in Scotland from 1936 onwards, Richmond was Professor of the Archaeology of the Roman Empire at Oxford at the time of his death. This collection of glass negatives relates to several sites, but particularly to work at the legionary fortress of Inchtuthil 1952–1965.

ALEXANDER A RITCHIE. Sketchbook

ALEXANDER A RITCHIE

Sketchbook 1830, Insc.: 'A. A. Ritchie, St John's Hill, Edinburgh'. Includes drawings after and designs for architectural orders: bas reliefs (many featuring putti with various attributes), ornamental borders, rinceau, etc., in sepia and watercolour. (A A Ritchie was a designer in James Ballantine's stained glass studio during the 1840s. See Robert T Skinner, *A Notable Family of Scots Printers*, Edinburgh, 1927, p.71).

JAMES RITCHIE (1850–1925)

Photographs and glass negatives of stone circles, standing stones and cup-marked stones in NE Scotland, 1901–17, taken by J Ritchie (father of Professor James Ritchie). Ritchie published several papers in the *Proceedings of the Society of Antiquaries of Scotland*, in at least one instance describing stone circles omitted by F R Coles in his surveys. All the articles were illustrated with photographs taken by Ritchie, most of which are in this collection.
Society of Antiquaries of Scotland MSS 41.

JAMES RITCHIE. Photograph by Ritchie of the Nine Stones, Garrol, Kincardine

J T ROCHEAD (1814–1878), Architect

(RIAS) Photographic portrait, Insc.; 'J T Rochead (1814–1878) Architect of the Wallace Monument presented by his grandson H Rochead Williamson FRIAS Architect, 2 Hill Street, Edinburgh'.

THE ROKEBY COLLECTION OF RAILWAY PHOTOGRAPHS, POSTCARDS AND PRINTED PLANS

A large collection of photographs, postcards and plans relating to railways and railway stations throughout Scotland, deposited in NMRS per NMR (England); collected and taken by the Rev. H D E Rokeby, Mundford Rectory, Thetford, Norfolk, between 1920 and 1968. Many of the photographs dating from the 1950s and 1960s were taken by Mr O Carter. With an Inventory of Stations arranged by County.
(NMRS Inventory 80).

ROSEBERY DRAWINGS

NMRS Photographic Survey of drawings in the collection of the Earl of Rosebery including: alternative proposals for Dalmeny House by William Atkinson c.1806, William Burn, Sir Jeffrey Wyattville 1814, and William Wilkins; a portfolio of designs for Dalmeny by William Wilkins c.1814; a folio of working drawings for

THE ROKEBY COLLECTION OF RAILWAY PHOTOGRAPHS, POSTCARDS AND PRINTED PLANS. Elgin Station, Moray

Dalmeny by William Wilkins 1819–1822; mid
19th-century designs for alterations at
Dalmeny; designs for Barnbougle Castle by
Robert Adam 1774; designs for additions to
Barnbougle by Robert Burn 1788; designs for
the gardens at Dalmeny by David Bryce 1854;
designs for furniture by James Morison 1830s;
designs for restoration of Barnbougle by
Sydney Mitchell and Wilson 1889; designs for
Rosebery House by Wardrop and Reid
1871–1879; designs for Rosebery House by
Sydney Mitchell and Wilson 1915; and estate
plans.
Copied 1978   (NMRS Inventory 113).

ROSEHAUGH

Sale Catalogue of contents. No date, c.1930.
Thomas Love & Sons, Perth. Illustrated.

ROSLIN ALBUM

Photograph album probably compiled by
Hezekiah Merrick of Eskhill House, Roslin,
owner of the Roslin Gunpowder Mills,
including several photographs of Roslin
Chapel (commissioned by Merrick from the
photographer John Thomson, custodian of the
Chapel c.1862) and many views in vicinity.

LANCELOT ROSS (1885–1956), Architect

(RIAS) A collection of exhibition drawings
and photographs by Lancelot Ross 1935–1955.

DR THOMAS ROSS (1839–1930), Architect

A collection of papers including: an Almanack
for 1870 with diary entries; a pocketbook
c.1870 with notes and addresses; family tree
and drafts and sketches for an illuminated
address to his parents on their 50th Wedding
Anniversary; two notebooks with draft entries
on Tarbert Castle, Fedderat, Smailholm,
Granton, Royston, Caroline Park, Gylen,
Dunstaffnage, Girniegoe, Balgonie,
Fountainhall, Midhope, Caerlaverock and
Fordel; sketchbook for 1898; letters to Ross
on research interests, including one of 1909
from R S Mylne; report for Marquess of Bute

*ROSLIN ALBUM. Roslin Chapel decorated
for Christmas 1862*

on an excavation at Castle Island, Mochrum;
certificate of conferral of Doctorate of Laws
1910; summons for the offence of sketching
Rossend Castle, 1915; report on Old Bridge of
Earn (for RCAHMS?); and a letter from Sir
Robert Lorimer requesting a private
consultation with Dr Ross about the design of
the Scottish National War Memorial, 'as now
modelled', prior to the meeting to discuss it by
the Ancient Monuments Board, and
expressing gratitude to Ross for his advice on
the design of the Thistle Chapel (with a copy
of Dr Ross's typewritten refusal).

Files of research notes and drafts of articles
for: Cakemuir Castle; Catcune Castle;
Crookston Castle; Dundas Castle; Loch-an
Eilean Castle; Evelick Castle; Fyvie Castle;
Fourmerkland Tower; Inverugie Castle; Kellie
Castle; Mearns Castle; Megginch Castle;
Muness Castle; Noltland Castle; Pitsligo Parish
Church; Ochiltree Castle; Ruthven Castle; The
Argyle Lodging, Stirling; Stobhall;
Torphichen; Traquair House; Yester Castle.

Manuscripts of Rhind Lectures on the
*Ecclesiastical Architecture of Scotland from the
12th to the 16th Century,* 1899 and the *History
of the Architecture of Scotland from the 12th to
the 17th Centuries,* 1902.
Society of Antiquaries of Scotland MSS 462.

Typescript, Insc.: 'Castellated and Domestic
Architecture of Scotland Additional notes by
Dr Thomas Ross,' with corrections and
additions to published text 1887–1892,
arranged by page numbers.

THE ROYAL COMMISSION ON THE
ANCIENT AND HISTORICAL MONUMENTS
OF SCOTLAND (RCAHMS)

Investigators' Notebooks: a series of
notebooks with survey notes made in the
preparation of the RCAHMS's County
Inventories beginning with Sutherland
1909–1990. Arranged by County for early

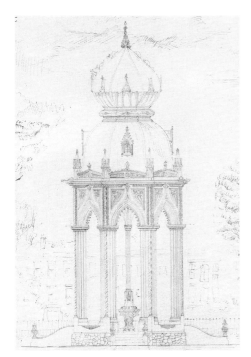

THE ROYAL INCORPORATION OF
ARCHITECTS IN SCOTLAND'S DRAWING
COLLECTION. *Caricature of a competition
drawing*

years but subsequently by Investigator,
individually indexed.

Emergency Survey 1940–46: Album of contact
prints of photographs taken throughout
Scotland against possible enemy destruction.
(This relates to the Emergency Survey
Typescript MS/36 of contemporary written
reports)

Marginal Land Surveys: between 1951 and
1958 the Commission undertook emergency
survey of marginal land in all parts of Scotland
where an expansion of agriculture and forestry
was expected.

Many earthworks were surveyed in detail for
the first time, and lists of monuments
discovered were published in the Selkirkshire
and Stirlingshire *Inventories*.

Press-cutting files relating to ancient
monuments and historic buildings throughout
Scotland.

THE ROYAL INCORPORATION OF ARCHITECTS IN SCOTLAND'S DRAWINGS COLLECTION

From the first abortive foundation in 1840, the
Institute of Scotland's Architects proposed to
include drawings in their library. A collection
of historic drawings was discovered in 1975 at
15 Rutland Square by Professor Alistair
Rowan during his researches for the David
Bryce Exhibition. This collection was
subsequently deposited with the NMRS. The
collecting of drawings received a new impetus
at the RIAS during the 1980s when it was
engaged in its pioneering survey of 1930s
drawings. Alarmed by the rate of destruction,
the RIAS decided to re-found its drawings
collection. The intention is to build up a
cabinet collection of representative drawings
by Scotland's architects primarily for
exhibition and educational purposes. In this
work the RIAS liaises closely with the NMRS,
(where the drawings are deposited in the
rooms devoted to the RIAS collection) and
the Scottish Record Office as well as other
relevant depositories in Scotland. The earliest
drawings in the collection are the scheme for
Hangingshaw by James Adam of 1766, and
there are also designs by W H Playfair, James
Gillespie Graham, William Burn, George
Meikle Kemp, R W Billings, George Shaw
Aitken, etc. (many noted individually in this
catalogue). Although twentieth-century
drawings have dominated the recent accessions
(with large collections like the James Miller
office drawings), many fine early drawings
have been added, of which the most important
is the David Neave album and two
presentation drawings for the Observatory on
Calton Hill, Edinburgh, by W H Playfair of
*c.*1820. The collection of student drawings is
one of its strongest areas.

THE ROYAL INCORPORATION OF ARCHITECTS IN SCOTLAND: THE INSTITUTE OF THE ARCHITECTS OF SCOTLAND

Bye-Laws, 1840. Xerox copy of original
document in possession of the Duke of
Buccleuch SRO GD/224/510/3/3.

Xerox copy of *Laws and Bye-Laws*, 1850.
Original in EAA Library.

Transactions Vol. 1, 1850–1851; Vol. 2
1851–1852; Vol. 3 1852–1854; Vol. 4, Parts
1–4, 1856–61.

Thomas Purdie, *Illustrations of an Essay on
Mural Decoration*, 1852. (These were too large
for inclusion in the *Transactions* and were
issued independently. The description of the
plates is in Vol. 2, pp. 249–251.

Transactions 1861–1869. The final volume of
the series is devoted to large-scale
lithographed plates of historic Scottish
architecture, with minimal descriptive
letterpress. (A composite set completed with
some xeroxed sections taken from the EAA
set.)

Proceedings 1851–1853. Incomplete series.
Xerox of EAA Library copy.

Reports of the Council of Management, Nos.
1–17, 1850–1860.
Xerox of EAA Library Copy.

Anon., *A Letter to the Members of the
Architectural Institute of Scotland by an
Ordinary Member*, 1858.
Xerox of Edinburgh Public Library copy.

Xerox copies of application for Student
Membership bound alphabetically 1928–1934.
Xerox copies of applications for Associate
Membership bound alphabetically 1928–1934.
Xerox copies of application for Fellowships
bound alphabetically 1930–1934.
(Like the RIBA Nomination papers these
include summaries of the applicant's career
and principal works.)
Originals with RIAS.

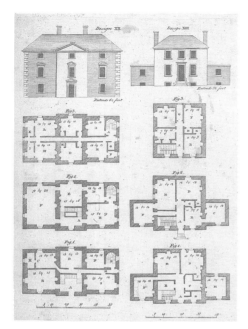

THE RUDIMENTS OF ARCHITECTURE.
Showing a design for Drummore House on left-hand side

THE RUDIMENTS OF ARCHITECTURE

The Rudiments of Architecture or the Young Workman's Instructor, 1778, Edinburgh. Printed for James Dickson and Charles Elliot.

One of the earliest Scottish architectural publications; this version is a re-issue of the designs in George Jameson, *Thirty Three Designs, with the Orders of Architecture, According to Palladio*, 1765, with the plates purged of Baroque elements.

ST FORT ALBUMS

Two photograph albums with a survey of St Fort House and estate, depicting interiors, outbuildings and vicinity 1893–1896.

ST MARTIN'S ABBEY DRAWINGS

NMRS Photographic Survey of designs for St Martin's Abbey by Peddie and Kinnear 1869, David Bryce 1860; and a plan of the Links Pottery by Robert Mitchell 1778.
Copied 1967   (NMRS Inventory 7).

THE SALTIRE SOCIETY

A large collection of entries, usually comprising an exhibition panel, for the Saltire Society's annual awards for Scottish Architecture 1956–1989.
Deposited by the Saltire Society.

SALTOUN HALL DRAWINGS

NMRS Photographic Survey of designs for Saltoun Hall including: designs and working drawings by William Burn 1818–1826; chimney-piece designs by David Ness, Leith Walk, Edinburgh; plans of cottages by Robert Burn 1804: designs for estate buildings by Robert Burn 1804; Drawing Room furniture-plan by Dowbiggin, London; design for Inveraray Old Castle by Alexander McGill c.1720; design for an octagon lodge by James Thin 1801; designs for Inveraray Church by John Adam; late 17th-century designs for a cube house; designs for Roseneath 1744 and 1747, etc. (This collection is now in the National Library of Scotland).
Copied 1968   (NMRS Inventory 4).

ROBERT WEIR SCHULTZ (1860–1951), Architect

Survey notes from a sketchbook relating to Crichton Peel and Sanquhar Church and related correspondence, 1896.

Typescript extracts from office papers in the Office of A B Waters relating to Robert Weir Schultz's Scottish commissions 1903–1913. *(NMRS Inventory 109).*

VIEWS IN SCOTLAND

Album entitled 'Views in Scotland' containing an alphabetically arranged collection of

'VIEWS IN SCOTLAND'. Interior of the Gallery at Kinfauns Castle

SIR GILBERT SCOTT. Carte-de-visite portrait

engravings, etchings, etc., bound-in, illustrating castles and country houses in Scotland c.1750–1840, including many rare views. Compiled c.1840.

SIR GILBERT SCOTT (1811–1878), Architect

A collection of working drawings for St Mary's Cathedral, Edinburgh and St Mary's Episcopal Cathedral, Glasgow.
Presented per NMR (England) 1967 and 1970.

Sixteen notebooks containing drafts for speeches and publications and sketches by Sir Gilbert Scott, presented to the Society of Antiquaries of Scotland by James Thomas Irvine. Accompanying letter from Scott to Irvine 11/4/1863 thanking him for a 'song, which is very pretty and well worthy of the fairies', and another letter, from Irvine, of July 1887 to Dr Joseph Anderson, Secretary of the Society of Antiquaries of Scotland, requesting their preservation in the SAS Library. Several of the notebooks Insc.: 'This notebook of my old Master Sir G G Scott RA was given to me by his son John O. Scott Oct 19 1886 J T Irvine'; also including a diary of an 'Architectural Tour on the Continent'.
Society of Antiquaries of Scotland MSS 380.

A collection of letters and biographical material relating to Sir Gilbert Scott compiled by James Thomas Irvine, including: letters from Scott to Irvine; letters from John Drayton Wyatt (who prepared many of Scott's office drawings) to Irvine; carte-de-visite photographs of Scott and his family; press cuttings relating to Scott's life and works; transcripts of Scott's writings, etc., 1862–1891.
Society of Antiquaries of Scotland MSS 398.

A collection of lithographs and photographs of buildings designed by Scott, and a few of his original sketch designs presented to the Society of Antiquaries of Scotland by J T Irvine, including: Chapel, St John's College, Cambridge; Lewisham Church, Kent; Lichfield Cathedral; sketch for a tomb at Lichfield Cathedral; sketch designs for choir-seats in Ely Cathedral; sketch designs for St Mary's Church, Mirfield; photographs of perspective designs for New India Office; and a sketch for Glasgow University Common Hall, 1857–1880.

SCOTTISH COLORFOTO LIMITED. View of Queen Victoria's Throne Room, Holyrood

Society of Antiquaries MSS 398 iii. (NMRS Inventory 108).

W SCHOMBERG SCOTT, Architect

The Office Drawings including designs for restoration schemes and new work throughout Scotland, including many designs for Monteviot 1957–1962. Drawings for work carried out for The National Trust for Scotland were transferred to NTS.

A collection of photographs by W Schomberg Scott of buildings designed by Reginald Fairlie.
Presented by W Schomberg Scott, 1977.

THE SCOTTISH BURGH SURVEY

Research files, index-cards, correspondence, draft reports, etc., prepared by the Scottish Burgh Survey, commissioned by the Ancient Monuments Division of the Department of the Environment. Sixty-three towns were covered by published reports.
Deposited by the Scottish Burgh Survey per Dr Eric Talbot, Department of Archaeology, University of Glasgow, 1984 (NMRS Inventory 159).

SCOTTISH COLORFOTO LIMITED, Photographers

NMRS Photographic Survey printed from negatives in the possession of the Scottish Colorfoto Ltd, Alexandria, during the late 1960s. This collection had inherited many plates from the Inglis Collection, who held the Royal Warrant. The collection therefore includes many views recording alterations to Holyrood Palace as well as progress and publicity photographs of many of the major public buildings in Edinburgh, including the Scottish National War Memorial in Edinburgh, and mainly dating from 1900–1939. The negatives were dispersed by auction in c.1985 and NMRS was subsequently able to save many of the original negatives for Holyrood. Copy prints, taken from the contact prints of the rest of the collection, can also be supplied. *Printed 1966–1970.*

SCOTTISH GAS

A very large collection of designs for gasworks throughout Scotland, and designs for subsequent alterations or additions mid 19th century–1965.
Deposited by Scottish Gas per Mr J Keith, 1984 (NMRS Inventory 155 parts 1–4).

THE SCOTTISH INDUSTRIAL ARCHAEOLOGY SURVEY

A large collection of over 1500 records carried out by the Scottish Industrial Archaeology Survey, founded in 1977, to carry out systematic surveys of significant industrial monuments in Scotland, and sponsored, initially, from rescue archaeology funds administered by the Department of the Environment. The Survey was merged with RCAHMS in 1985, and its staff and archive became permanent members of the Commission's staff and organisation. The records have now been incorporated in NMRS and a *Catalogue of Records: Scottish Industrial Archaeology Survey 1977–85* was published by RCAHMS in 1989, listing the surveys both by Region and District and also thematically (e.g. 'Ceramics', 'Town Gas', 'Windmills'). This also includes a list of the Survey's Thematic Studies including: Suspension Bridges; Hand-Cranes; Horizontal Watermills; Vertical Watermills; Windmills and Wind-Engines; 'Dickie' Windpumps, etc.

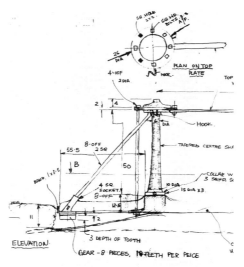

THE SCOTTISH INDUSTRIAL ARCHAEOLOGY SURVEY. Sketch survey of horse-gin, South Killellan Farm, Southend, Argyll

THE SCOTTISH NATIONAL BUILDINGS RECORD

Files of papers relating to establishment of SNBR (SRO MW/6/1 SC20300/1) and formation of Scottish Council 1940–1953.

Minute Book 9th May 1941–26th March 1954. (SRO SC 20300/3).

George Scott-Moncrieff (Secretary), *The Buildings of Scotland:* a short history of architecture in Scotland compiled for the National Buildings Record, Scottish Council, 1944. Cover sketch by J S Richardson. Apparently written for the exhibition of the SNBR's collection of measured drawings in Glasgow Art Gallery 1943.

Cash Books and Accounts 1941–1953 (SRO SC 20300/2).

Annual Reports May 1941–1945. (SRO SC 29037/1).

THE SCOTTISH NATIONAL BUILDINGS RECORD. Cover of war-time Glasgow Exhibition brochure

Annual Reports 1955–1966. (SRO SC 29037/2).

Correspondence 1954–1958, with carbon copies of outgoing letters interleaved.

SCOTTISH URBAN ARCHAEOLOGICAL TRUST (SUAT)

Collection of excavation archives comprising drawings, notebooks, reports, colour slides, photographs and negatives of excavations in towns throughout Scotland, including: Canal Street, Perth, 1978; Castle Street, Inverness, 1979; and Kirkwall, Orkney, 1978. Developed from the Urban Archaeology Unit, SUAT was established in 1982 to undertake excavation and research into the origins and development of towns in Scotland.
Deposited by SUAT.

SCOTT MORTON & CO., Architectural Woodworkers

Press-cutting album c.1900–1966. Xerox of original in possession of Mrs Hardie (grand-daughter of founder, William Scott Morton). Includes copy of liquidation sale catalogue Tuesday 25 October 1966, Thomas Hill and Co., Edinburgh.
Copied 1986.

SEGGIEDEN

NMRS survey of private collections, inventory of estate papers, including letters from William Burn, September 1825.
(NMRS Inventory 5).

JAMES SHEARER (1881–1962), Architect

A large collection of personal and office papers relating to the life and works of this architect, including: family photographs; an extensive collection of notebooks and sketchbooks containing his reminiscences, notes for jobs in hand and drafts for lectures, publications and literary projects; a series of Memo Books 1948–1962 with jottings on each day's activities and expenses; office files relating to jobs including works for the Carnegie Trust Dunfermline, (Library, Birthplace and Memorial Museum), Hydro Electric Board, etc; press-cutting files on varied subjects; folders of photographs of executed works (including restoration of Brucefield House, Aberfoyle Pavilion, etc.); typescripts of publications and lectures, including an appreciation of the architect, H L Honeyman; printed literature relating to the work of the Carnegie Trust in Dunfermline; an album of photographs recording a visit to France and Italy in 1956; a file of letters of congratulation on the award of his OBE, etc.
Presented by his family per Roger Emerson, 1987.

REV. JOHN SIME (1790–1864), Antiquarian

Album, Insc: 'MEMORABILIA JOn. SIME EDINr. 1840' Containing a large collection of antiquarian sketches, measured surveys and

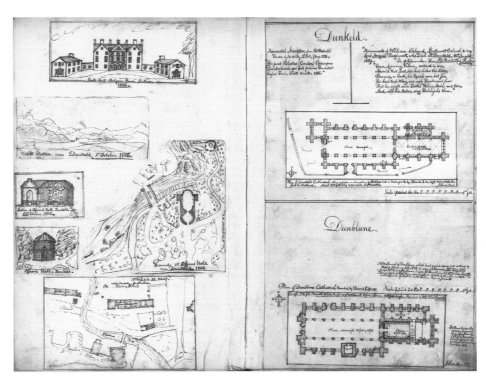

REV. JOHN SIME. Page from his 'Memorabilia'

engravings of Scottish and English castles, churches and towns. Sime was ultimately Chaplain to Trinity College Hospital in Edinburgh and, after its demolition, James Gillespie's Hospital. He was an enthusiastic antiquarian, and the album reflects his wide interests and shows evidence of his early architectural training. It incorporates an inked-up early sketchbook of c.1804–1807. Surveys include in Scotland: the Lawnmarket, Edinburgh; Edinburgh University; Craigmillar Castle; Borthwick Castle; the Border Abbeys; St Andrews; Cowdenknowes House; Culross Abbey House; Dunfermline; Perth Town Churches and a plan of Pittenweem, etc. Surveys in England include: Carlisle Cathedral; Walwick Grange; Alnwick; Warkworth; Norham; Ford Castle and Church, etc.

Folder, Insc.: 'Scrolls and Plans J Sime', including a large collection of architectural designs, antiquarian surveys and engravings, etc., by John Sime. The designs include: 'Plans for Repairing the Canongate Church 30th Nov 1815 Charles XII', an unidentified item, a church 1810, etc. The surveys include: Doocots at Valleyfield copied from the plans; Melrose Abbey; Borthwick Castle; St Andrews, Durham; Moray House, Canongate.

The collection also comprises a number of architectural drawings collected by Sime, including: studies of the orders; a perspective view of a church like St Pauls, Covent Garden; and a design for an 'Adam' chimney-piece collected by Sime.
(The John Douglas drawings (see above) were extracted from this folder).

Folder. Insc.: 'Roman Antiquities &c, Architecture, Scotch Scenery' Including a large collection of engravings of architectural and antiquarian subjects and Sime's own design for 'The Church of St Ninian, North Leith'. The latter is evidently a competition entry as his own name 'John Sime at Mr David Sime's head of Lawnmarket Edinburgh' has been concealed by a flap secured with sealing wax. The Sime Collection was presented by the Company of Merchants of the City of Edinburgh 1985, who have retained the original drawings for *Edinburgh in Olden Time* and William Douglas's survey perspectives of Trinity College Hospital.

ARCHIBALD SIMPSON. Portrait after James Giles

ARCHIBALD SIMPSON (1790–1847), Architect

Portrait. Engraving (two copies: NMRS and RIAS) after James Giles, RSA, published 1849.

Dr W. DOUGLAS SIMPSON (*d.*1968)

A collection of papers including: notes of Duirinish Old Church 1943; a letter from C B Balfour concerning the history of Balgonie Castle 1896; a letter to Simpson from A R

JAMES SKENE OF RUBISLAW. Sketch of Pictish stone, Aberlemno, Angus

Borthwick (no date) about Borthwick Castle recording its restoration in 1892 and present use; a collection of proof sheets from MacGibbon and Ross's *Castellated and Domestic Architecture of Scotland;* and a large collection of photographs.

Typescript article *The Nunnery on Iona*, uncorrected draft.
Deposited by J G Dunbar, 1983.

JAMES SKENE OF RUBISLAW (1775–1864)

Portfolio of drawings of sculptured monuments in Scotland dated 1832. Most of the drawings are executed in pen and brown ink, with or without a brown wash, and are annotated in brown ink. Some of the drawings illustrate stones which have now disappeared.
Society of Antiquaries of Scotland MSS 464.

JOHN SMITH (1781–1852), Architect

A collection of documents and ledgers relating to Smith's architectural practice and business interests, including: annual bundles of vouchers addressed to John Smith for subcontracted work, e.g. 'Aberdeen Cast Iron Foundry' and house-painters etc. 1816–1832; a ledger recording timber used and sold 10 July 1817–24 December 1818; two ledgers recording hours worked and consequent payments to workmen; cash-books arranged by jobs 1807; two ledgers recording ironmongery, etc., supplied by Allan and Simpson 1827–1828 and 1830–1832; a ledger recording work for Lord Forbes of Putachie; a ledger recording miscellaneous work in Aberdeen and elsewhere, including Marischal College, Court House, Udny Chapel, Craigievar, Ellon Chapel, etc., two 'Abstract Books' recording jobs 2 January 1829–September 1830 and 1830–1832; ledger, Insc. 'Material Book,' commencing 16 May 1822–24 July 1828, listing timbers, etc., used by job and client.

THE SMITHS OF DARNICK, Architects and Builders

NMRS Survey of private collections. Miscellaneous papers including: photographs of sketches of details of Melrose Abbey by John Smith; typescript transcript of diary of John Smith 1812–1854, with attached family tree and transcripts of family letters; xerox of engagement diary for 1822; xerox of engagement diary for 1864; xeroxes of tours to Buxton 1839 and 1848; xerox of copy letter book 1850–58, concerned with clearing estate; xeroxes of a paper on Whinstone Construction printed for the *Transactions of the Institute of British Architects* 1835–36, and the contract for Bowhill House 1831; photographic copies of plans for house built by and subsequently occupied by the family at Darnick.
Copied 1986.

SIR BASIL SPENCE. Design for garage at Causewayside, Edinburgh

MRS J STEWART SMITH SKETCHES. View of Cowgate, Edinburgh

MRS J STEWART SMITH SKETCHES

A collection of sketches recording picturesque architectural subjects in the Old Town of Edinburgh, many dated 1868, (including Holyrood, and many subjects in Canongate, Lawnmarket, High Street, and the interior of a house in Cant's Close). (Published as plates of J Stewart Smith, *Historic Stones and Stories of Bygone Edinburgh*) 1924.
Purchased by SNBR from Mr Waddell, Portobello, 1952.

SOCIETY OF ANTIQUARIES OF SCOTLAND MANUSCRIPTS

The archaeological material in this collection contains an exciting range of antiquarian manuscripts, drawings and photographs. Some of the material has appeared in the *Proceedings* of the Society, but many items are unpublished. A selection of some of the more important components of this collection have been singled out and described in greater detail.
Deposited by the Society of Antiquaries of Scotland, 1975.

SOMERVILLE POSTCARD COLLECTION

A large collection of postcards depicting Scottish Castles, formed by Mrs H Somerville of Edinburgh, and associated notebooks with historical information on each castle *c.*1930s–1940s.
Presented by her family.

SORN CASTLE DRAWINGS

NMRS Photographic Survey of drawings for Sorn Castle in the possession of Watson, Salmond and Gray, Architects, Glasgow, including: designs for additions by William Railton 1862 and two schemes for additions by David Bryce 1863.
Copied 1980 (NMRS Inventory 119).

SOUTHFIELD HOUSE, EDINBURGH

A portfolio of designs for Southfield House, by John Chesser 1874.

SIR BASIL SPENCE (1907–1976), Architect

A collection of exhibition and presentation drawings including: competition entry for RIBA Soane Medallion 1931–32, 'A National Library in a Capital'; design for a house at Easter Belmont and a garage at Causewayside, Edinburgh, 1933; design for cottage and shop on Colonsay 1934; design for a house on the Comiston Estate, Edinburgh, for Mr and Mrs MacWhannel 1934; design for Broughton Place 1935; undated designs for Cleghorn's, Princes Street, Edinburgh; cottage at Colinton for James Allan; a Church, etc.
Deposited by Kinninmonth Collections.

SPRINGBANK MILLS, DUNBLANE

Nine account books relating to Springbank Mills 1857–1891.
Deposited by Mr Orton, Manager, Springbank Mills, 1980.

SPRINGWOOD PARK DRAWINGS. Design for entrance front by James Gillespie Graham

SPRINGWOOD PARK DRAWINGS

A large collection of designs for House, Mausoleum and Estate buildings including: a series of alternative presentation drawings by James Gillespie Graham; watercolour perspectives of proposed drawing rooms c.1820; designs for additions by Brown and Wardrop c.1850; furniture designs; design for a Keeper's Lodge by Wm R Gray; fireplace designs; designs for home farm 1880s, cottages, Maisondieu Steading; additions to Heiton Mains; design for cottages at Maxwellheugh; plans of Easter Softlaws Farmhouse, etc.

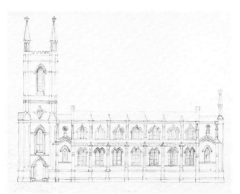

F. STANLEY. Sketchbook; design for a church

F STANLEY (Student Architect?)

Sketchbook, Insc.: 'Architecture F Stanley January 1853' with juvenile, but improving, designs for villas, churches, etc., and a survey (or design?) drawing for rising shutters for protecting shop windows.
Presented with William Notman Collection, 1981.

GEORGE STEWART'S SKETCHES

A collection of pencil sketches including: Borthwick Castle; Castle Farm and Wallace Monument (Renfrewshire); Crookston Castle; Doune Castle; Dunbar Castle; Dunderave Castle; Dundonald Castle; Dunolly Castle; Dunstaffnage Castle; Fotheringay Mound; Glasgow Green; Gylen Castle; Iona Abbey; Kelso Abbey; Kilmartin Castle; Queen Mary's House, Jedburgh; Loch Leven Castle; Knock Hill Fort, Largs; Neidpath Castle; Cairn and Stone Circle, Newbridge. Many dated 1867.
Presented by his great-nephew J G Stewart Macphail, 1968.

DR MARGARET E C STEWART (1907–1986)

This collection comprises drawings, photographs, notebooks, reports and correspondence from at least fifteen major excavations and surveys throughout Perthshire, undertaken 1950–74 by M E C Stewart, a student of Professor V G Childe. It includes Allt na Moine Buidhe deserted settlement, 1969–70; and Moncreiffe House stone circle 1974.

STOBO CASTLE DRAWINGS

NMRS Photographic Survey of designs for Stobo Castle, including preliminary designs and contract drawings by Archibald and James Elliot 1804.
Copied 1971   (NMRS Inventory 35).

STONEFIELD CASTLE DRAWINGS

NMRS Photographic Survey of designs for Stonefield Castle (formerly Barmore Castle) by William Henry Playfair 1836–1840.
Copied 1976   (NMRS Inventory 68).

ALEXANDER STRANG (1916–1984), Architect

A collection of student drawings by Alexander Strang during his training at Glasgow School of Architecture 1935–1938, including: studies of the orders, projects, and designs for a National Theatre prepared for the Rowand Anderson Studentship; and presentation panels depicting historic architecture.
Presented by his son, Charles Strang, 1986.

Notebook with notes on Building Construction Lectures at Glasgow School of Architecture 1936–1937.
Presented by Charles Strang.

STUART'S GRANOLITHIC STONE CO. LTD

Stuart's Granolithic Souvenir, 1901.
6 Torphichen Place, Edinburgh. Illustrated with views of works, products and buildings utilising the granolithic system, including Waverley Station Hotel, and Jenner's Warehouse, Princes Street, Edinburgh, and view of Showrooms.

*STUART'S GRANOLITHIC STONE CO.
LTD. Catalogue advertisement*

SIR JOHN SUMMERSON (*b.*1904)

Taped recording of Sir John Summerson's
paper read at the Robert Adam 250th
Conference organised by the Extra Mural
Department of Edinburgh University 1978.
Presented by Basil Skinner, 1989.

ROBERT G SUTHERLAND, Decorator

Papers of Robert G Sutherland, Painter and
Decorator, 109 Bellevue Road, Edinburgh
*c.*1900–1930, including: sketches for
decorations and a scheme for a picture house;
accounts; wallpaper samples; cuttings and
printed source material; stencils; catalogues of
decorating firms; and a Ridgely graining roller.
(NMRS Inventory 135).

T SCOTT SUTHERLAND, Architect

(RIAS) An album of press-cuttings recording
the business and social activities of this
Aberdeen architect and city councillor
1930–1960.

TAIN MUSEUM PLANS

Plans from Tain Museum deposited in NMRS,
including: contract drawing for Tain Water
Works 1870; designs for arrangements of
mural monuments in St Duthus Church, Tain
1881; designs for Carnegie Library, Tain 1902;
design for Tain Public Shambles 1884, etc.
(NMRS Inventory 150).

TARBOLTON AND OCHTERLONY, Harold
Ogle Tarbolton 1869–1947, Sir Matthew M
Ochterlony d. 1946, Architects

A collection of photographs from the firm of
Harold Ogle Tarbolton (1869–1947), and Sir
Matthew M Ochterlony (*d.*1946), including:
family photographs; an album of architectural
press-cuttings; photographs of art and
architectural subjects from an Italian Tour;
photographs of unidentified works in Scotland,
including furniture and church fittings
photographed in Scott Morton's workshops;
photographs of contemporary English
buildings; a photograph of a 'House in
Colinton Road' in course of construction;
photographs of a model for St Bride's Church
and a letter from J W Singer and Sons Ltd
Metalworkers *re* a lectern designed by Messrs
Hay and Henderson, Architects.
*Provenance: thought to have come through a
member of the Henderson family.*

THE TAY BRIDGE

NMRS Photographic Survey of a collection of
photographs of the Tay Bridge during
construction in 1876 and after the disaster of
1879 with technical notes by G D Hay,
RCAHMS.
Copied 1986   (NMRS Inventory 170).

HAROLD RAMSAY TAYLOR (1864–1922),
Architect

Album of press-cuttings, etc., compiled by H
R Taylor of Lessels and Taylor, Architects,
Edinburgh, 1895–1917, including: Public
Library, Dundee Street; alterations at
Boroughloch Brewery; Stockbridge Branch
Library; Stirling Public Library; Leith Walk
Library; and designs for completing Chambers
Street. Taylor was also an inventor, and there
are details of his railway-signalling
improvements and a periscope intended for
the trenches.

PROFESSOR ALEXANDER THOM
(1894–1985)

An important modern collection of
archaeological drawings comprising *c.*600
original survey drawings and *c.*100 notebooks
of stone circles, standing stones and
alignments throughout Scotland, England,
Wales and France, 1938–78. An engineer by
profession, Thom's interest in prehistoric
megalithic sites developed as a hobby but
became a second career, resulting in this
collection and over 120 publications. Copies of
the latter, many annotated by Thom, are also
held in the NMRS.

*CAPTAIN FREDERICK W L THOMAS.
Section drawing of Dun Telve, Glenelg,
Inverness*

CAPTAIN FREDERICK W L THOMAS
(*d.*1885), Royal Navy

While a lieutenant in command of the survey
vessel 'Woodlark', engaged in the Admiralty
survey of Orkney, Shetland and the Western
Isles, Thomas sketched, surveyed, took notes
and photographed numerous upstanding
monuments. His notes, written in HMSO
Naval Stores logs, formed the basis of his

articles in the *Proceedings of the Society of Antiquaries of Scotland* and *Archaeologia Scotica*. He continued his research in Edinburgh, having drawings and plans by H Dryden (held by the Society of Antiquaries of Scotland) traced and copied by W Galloway.
Society of Antiquaries of Scotland MSS 29, 33–38.

TRAPRAIN LAW

The visitors' book from the excavations in 1921–2 by J E Cree and A O Curle, includes signatures of A T Curle (son of A O Curle), J S Richardson, C S T Calder, various members of the Cree family and visitors from as far away as New Zealand.

SIR FRANCIS TRESS BARRY. Monument to Tress Barry at Nybster, Caithness

SIR FRANCIS TRESS BARRY (1825–1907)

Collection of original excavation photographs, sketch drawings by John Nicolson and correspondence, mainly with Dr Joseph Anderson, relating to the research and excavations undertaken by Sir Francis Tress Barry during his visits to Keiss Castle, Caithness. Tress Barry became interested in archaeology, collecting artefacts and excavating about twenty sites, mainly brochs,

between 1890 and 1904. Apart from a paper read to the Society of Antiquaries of London in 1899 describing the discovery and excavation of several brochs, and an outline by Joseph Anderson in the *Proceedings of the Society of Antiquaries of Scotland* in 1901, Barry unfortunately did not publish his work, and this collection provides the only record of his research in the NMRS.
Society of Antiquaries of Scotland MSS 187, 291, 410, 470.

THOMS AND WILKIE (Patrick Thoms *d.* 1946), Architects

(RIAS) The surviving Office Drawings, including many designs for houses and villas in Dundee and district, and Newtyle House for Sir Charles Cayzer Bart 1904–1924.

(RIAS) Photograph album illustrating public buildings, country houses, villas and church furnishings designed by the architects.

TOUCH HOUSE DRAWINGS

NMRS Photographic Survey of plans for Touch House, including: 18th-century designs, one dated 1747 and signed by 'James Steinson'; drawings for Inveraray Castle; designs for additions to Touch by James Gillespie Graham 1809; and plans for proposed additions by Sir William Burroughs, Bart. *c.*1815.
Copied 1973   (NMRS Inventory 48).

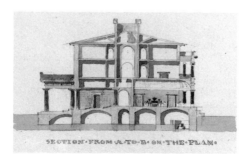

TOWNLEY HALL. Design by James Playfair

TOWNLEY HALL (Ireland, Co. Louth)

Portfolio. Insc.: 'Design for a House for (...) Balfour Esq'; S. and d.: 'James Playfair Architect Rome 1792; Elevations, plans and sections.
Presented by Professor Mitchell, 1985.

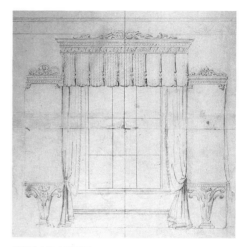

THE TROTTER ALBUMS OF GEORGE POTTS. Scheme for the drawing room at Mavisbank

THE TROTTER ALBUMS OF GEORGE POTTS

Two albums containing a large collection of sketches, presentation drawings, working drawings and a few contract drawings (many at full size) for architectural woodwork and furniture by Trotter of Edinburgh, the city's leading furniture maker. Many of the schemes in the Gothic style were executed for the architect James Gillespie Graham, to the design of A W N Pugin. Including designs for most of the firm's major commissions: at Taymouth Castle; George Heriot's Hospital; Floors Castle; Mavisbank; Crom Castle, Northern Ireland; and many unidentified. The volumes also include source material used by the firm in their design activities and a collection of tracings after designs by George

Bullock. The papers were probably salvaged by George Potts, who was one of the employees who entered into a partnership as Potts, Cairnie and Ray to continue the firm when Charles Trotter (son of the founder, William) withdrew c.1850. The partnership went into sequestration c.1860 and was wound up. The drawings date from c.1815–1860. See Ian Gow, 'New Light on Late Trotter' *Country Life*, August 11, 1988, pp. 100–103. *Purchased 1985 with the aid of a 50 per cent grant from the National Art Collections Fund.*

TURRIFF, 4 Castle Street and 2 Queen's Road

Photograph album with a comprehensive record of these buildings, including sketches, wallpaper and floorcovering samples, 1980. *Presented by Department of Roads, Grampian Regional Council, 1981.*

TYNECASTLE COMPANY

Catalogue. *Supplement, 1908, New Designs for Ceilings, Friezes, Dados, Panels, Etc.* Photographically illustrated.

Catalogue. *Undercut Tynecastle* No date, c.1910. Photographically illustrated.

Catalogue. *Canvas, Vellum, Textures, Compo, Wood Mouldings Adaptable and Fibrous Plaster.* No date, but inscribed '1923'. Photographically illustrated.

Catalogue. *Canvas, Vellum, Textures, Leathers, Mosaics Wood Mouldings* 1900 Albert Works, Murieston Road, Edinburgh. Covered with gilded Tynecastle canvas. Photographically illustrated. *Purchased 1984.*

Catalogue. *Supplement to Catalogue of 1900,* 1902 Albert Works, Murieston Road, Edinburgh. Photographically illustrated. *Purchased 1984.*

Catalogue. *Adams.* (Supplement to Catalogues of 1900 and 1902) 1903. Albert Works,

Murieston Road, Edinburgh. Photographically illustrated. Designs for ceilings in Adam style. *Purchased 1984.*

Catalogue. *Tynecastle Relief Decorations.* No date, c.1930. Photographically illustrated.

STANISLAW TYROWICZ

Preparatory survey notes for measured drawings by S Tyrowicz, including: Arniston House; Craigie Hall; Haddington House; Melville House; Pinkie House; Signet Library, Edinburgh; Smeaton Hepburn; The Binns; and Tulliebardine Church. (Draughtsman SNBR; emigrated to South Africa 1952).

VIKING AND EARLY SETTLEMENT ARCHAEOLOGICAL RESEARCH PROJECTS (VESARP)

Archive comprising excavation and survey drawings, notebooks, photographs and negatives from all VESAR projects, under the direction of C D Morris from 1975–85, including Brough of Deerness monastic settlement.

J JEFFREY WADDELL (1876–1941)

Five sketchbooks of architectural subjects and details; no date, but earliest probably compiled while a schoolboy. *Presented by John Smith and Son, Booksellers, Glasgow.*

A large collection of miscellaneous architectural papers including: personal papers and household accounts; papers relating to his architectural office; miscellaneous papers relating to architectural works c.1918–1922 (including Castle Picture House, New Cumnock; Camps Works Motherwell; Paragon Picture House, Cumberland Street, Glasgow; Park UF Church Uddingston; work at Provand's Lordship, Glasgow; UF Church Eglinton Street, Glasgow; Newlandsfield Bleach Works, Pollokshaws, Glasgow; House for James Bishop, Barncluith, Lanarkshire;

J JEFFREY WADDELL. Bookplate

"Ferniehurst", 17 Pollok Road, Shawlands, Glasgow; Maxwell Picture House, Main Street, Pollokshaws, Glasgow; West Parish Church, Rutherglen; Bedford Picture House, Eglinton Street, Glasgow; Dalmarnock Picture House, 68 Bath Street, Glasgow; Cinema, Moredaunt Street, Glasgow; Grove Picture House, New City Road, Glasgow); eleven notebooks and miscellaneous papers relating to antiquarian researches and publications; photographic portrait of J Jeffrey Waddell; and family photographs. *Found at Caldergrove House, home of J Jeffrey Waddell and presented to NMRS per Miss Anne Riches, Historic Buildings and Monuments, SDD.*

Album containing press-cuttings of articles on local antiquities, architecture and topography by J Jeffrey Waddell, published by *The Hamilton Advertiser*, 1910, including a series

J JEFFREY WADDELL. Design for an unidentified church

"The Baronial Residences of Lanarkshire'. With additional cuttings by other authors relating to local matters.

Bookplate depicting three Muses, one with dividers, and a circular domed temple.

DR DAVID M WALKER, Principal Inspector of Historic Buildings

Albums of pencil thumbnail sketches of the architecture of Perthshire and Kincardineshire, grouped on individual pages by parishes. Used as an aide-memoire while compiling the Lists of Buildings of Architectural and Historic Interest for these counties.
Deposited by Dr David M Walker, 1983.

Letters to SNBR concerning Dr Walker's researches on Scottish architects; illustrated with sketches, 1954–1960.

Draft entries for a Biographical Dictionary of Scottish Architects.
Presented by Dr David M Walker.

WARREN DRAWINGS

NMRS Photographic Survey of a collection of early 18th-century drawings in the possession of John Warren, including: designs for Saltoun Hall and estate buildings; Brunstane House, property in the Canongate; designs for

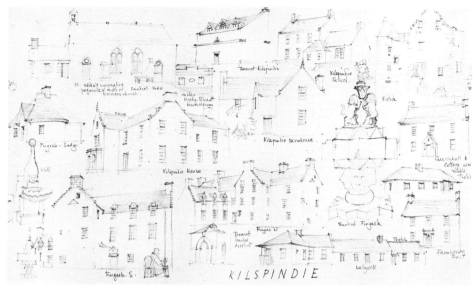

DR DAVID M WALKER. Record sketches of Kilspindie

Inveraray Old Castle by Alexander McGill; Inveraray Estate Buildings; Argyll House, London, etc.
Copied 1972   (NMRS Inventory 46).

JOHN WATHERSTON AND SONS, Builders

A large collection of drawings in the possession of the Edinburgh builders, John Watherston and Sons *c.*1857–1912. Includes many feuing plans and plans submitted for tenders as well as earlier architectural drawings acquired in the course of business, e.g. James Craig's surveys of Mount Stuart 1777. Including: Ancrum House; Borthwick Castle; Drummore House; Douglas Gardens and Rothesay Terrace, etc., Edinburgh; Duddingston House; The Hirsel; Mount Stuart House; Prestonpans Church; Sunlaws House, etc.
Presented by John Watherston and Sons, 1973   (NMRS Inventory 131).

JOHN WATHERSTON AND SONS. Design for rebuilding Sunlaws House

WEMYSS BAY MEMORIAL CHURCH ALBUM

Photograph album, Insc.: 'Memorial Church Wemyss Bay' *c.*1879, recording building and dedication of church built by George Burns in memory of his wife including photographs by T and R Annan, Glasgow of the completed Church, the Parsonage and Wemyss House ('The Seat of George Burns from 1860') and lithographs of the designs for the Church.

WEMYSS DRAWINGS

NMRS Photographic Survey of designs for the Wemyss Estates including: a portfolio of surveys of the Wemyss Estates by William Blackadder 1821; designs and working drawings for Gosford House by Robert Adam 1790–1791 (many at full size); and many designs for estate buildings.
Copied 1981 (NMRS Inventory 148).

NMRS Photographic Survey of a portfolio of survey drawings of the Wemyss estates by John Ainslie 1807.
Copied 1986 (NMRS Inventory 157).

WEMYSS MUNIMENTS

Extracts from the Estate accounts 1749–1808 recording payments for buildings, architects and craftsmen for work at Amisfield, Gosford, etc.
Surveyed 1984 (NMRS Inventory 148).

WESTERN ISLES ALBUM

Photograph album, Insc.: 'With the Churches Commission July 1906', probably compiled by the Rev. A Lee, recording a visitation by a party of United Free Church members. Lee was their Mission Superintendent.

THE WHIM

NMRS Photographic Survey of a collection of plans for additions to the The Whim and designs for offices and the stables. Attributed to David Henderson (fl.1765–c.1787), Architect.
Copied 1990.

JOHN FORBES WHITE, Photographer

A collection of 68 paper negatives and prints of King's College and St Machar's Aberdeen; the Brig of Balgownie; Holyrood Abbey; Kirkwall Cathedral and the Bishop's Palace; and an unidentified thatched cottage 1855–1857.
Presented to SNBR by the Edinburgh

JOHN FORBES WHITE. Kirkwall Cathedral

Photographic Society per Mr W Forbes Boyd, President, 1948.

Notebook, Insc.: 'Notes John Forbes White' with list of architectural photographic subjects.

WHYTOCK AND REID, Cabinetmakers and Upholsterers.

Xerox copy of *'Hand-Book of Estimates for House Furnishing'*. No date, c.1870

Xerox copy of 'Job Book' with dates of major commissions 1892–1939.

Xerox copy of 'Estimate Book', 1910–1924.
Copied 1985.

WILLIAM WILLIAMSON, Architect

Photograph album, Insc.: William Williamson Architect', with photographs of buildings designed by Williamson in Kirkcaldy and vicinity c.1900, including: The Croft; Burgh Buildings; Station Hotel; Electric Generating Station; High Street Buildings; House at Kincardine-on-Forth; Kirkcaldy Elementary School; Zion Mills, County Tyrone, Ireland; Royal Bank Buildings, Kirkcaldy; H W Renny House, Dundee; Station Hotel Ballroom, Kirkcaldy; 'Princess Ena'—a ship; Public Library, Burntisland; Labour Homes,

WILLIAM WILLIAMSON. Photograph album

Inverkeithing; Raith Rovers Football Ground; and St Johns Church.

CHARLES WILSON (1810–1863), Architect

The office drawings. A large collection of designs by Charles Wilson for buildings in Glasgow and the South West of Scotland, including: layout of Kelvingrove Park 1854; Trinity College Church 1855; Free Church Training College 1855–1856; St John's Episcopal Church, Oban 1863; Park Circus, Glasgow 1854; and many designs for churches, public buildings and houses.
Presented by John S Boyd, 1954.

Specification for buildings designed by Charles Wilson: Property on East Corner of Adelphi Street and Thistle Street for Proprietors of Hutcheson's Hospital 1838; Shops in Sussex Place for Proprietors of Hutcheson's Hospitals 1838; and a New Toll House at Muir House Toll Bar 1844.

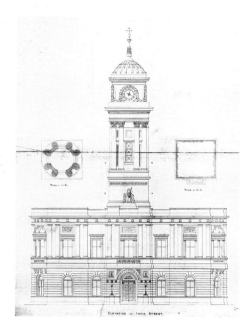

CHARLES WILSON. Office drawings; design for Free Church College, Glasgow

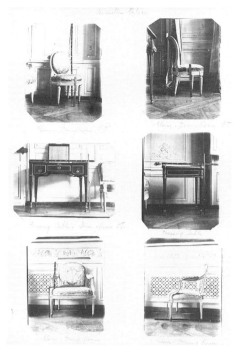

JOHN WILSON. Album: photographs of furniture at Petit Trianon

GEORGE WASHINGTON WILSON (1823–1893), Photographer

A collection of photographs by George Washington Wilson, formerly in the collection of Mr Fenton Wyness, Aberdeen.
Deposited by Mr and Mrs Murray (NMRS Inventory 70).

JOHN WILSON (d. 1959), Architect

A collection of miscellaneous papers including: A photograph album of family photographs.

An album of press-cuttings relating to hospital planning, housing, slum clearance, research on economical building construction for mass housing, etc. (many commenting on writings and speeches by John Wilson when Chief Architect to the Department of Health in Scotland and dated 1922–1939).

A folder of letters of congratulation on the award of the OBE, 1941, from professional colleagues and personal friends.

A letter from George Wallace, Department of Health, Edinburgh, thanking John Wilson for the gift to the Department of a drawing of the Petit Trianon 1943.

Two Photograph albums, *c*1910.
1 Comprising photographs of Versailles, Petit Trianon and its furnishings, Rouen, Fontainebleau, Paris, etc. Many taken by Wilson but including commercial views. (See Arnot and J Wilson, *The Petit Trianon*, 1907.)
2 Including photographs of sites in France; photographs of working drawings by George Washington Browne (including Miss

Cranston; 91 and 93 Buchanan Street, Glasgow; and 31 and 32 Princes Street Edinburgh); photographs of sketches of Scottish Castles, etc., by Browne; unidentified newly-erected houses and villas, etc; Wells; Oxford; Hopetoun, etc.

WIMPEY ALBUM

Photograph album, Insc.: 'Multi Storey Flats and Maisonette Blocks designed for Scottish Local Authorities by the Wimpey Organisation, Geo. Wimpey and Co. Ltd, Barnton Grove, Edinburgh 4', 1956–1960, including housing in Edinburgh, Glasgow, Perth, Dundee, Dunfermline, Motherwell, Wishaw, Hamilton, Rutherglen and Irvine.
Presented by Clydesdale District Council Museum, 1987.

WOODSIDE HOUSE ALBUM

Photograph album compiled by Miss Murray of Woodside House, Blairgowrie, 1883, with a survey of Woodside House and gardens; Lintrose Estate; 4 Torphichen Street and 12 Howard Place, Edinburgh; Perth Station; the Bazaar at Coupar-Angus; Meigle House, etc.

FENTON WYNESS, Architect

A collection of measured drawings by Fenton Wyness (*c*.1925) and George Watt (1883–1886), including: Crathes Castle; Craigievar Castle; Gight Castle; House of Schivas; Fortrose Cathedral; Beauly Priory; Elgin Cathedral; Kinloss Abbey, etc.

E R YERBURY AND SON, Photographers

NMRS Survey of late 19th- and 20th-century photographs taken by Yerbury of subjects in Edinburgh and London.
Copied 1971 (NMRS Inventory 33).

KIRK YETHOLM CHURCH DRAWINGS

NMRS Photographic Survey of designs for

WIMPEY ALBUM. Royston Road, Glasgow

Kirk Yetholm Church by John and Thomas
Smith 1835.
Copied 1972   (NMRS Inventory 44).

ALISON YOUNG

Encouraged by Sir Lindsay Scott, Alison
Young excavated and photographed various
sites throughout Scotland, including Monzie
kerb cairn 1938, and Dun Cuier, Barra broch
1953–5. Her particular interest was pottery,
unfortunately not represented in this
collection, which comprises photographs,
negatives and some excavation drawings.

G P K YOUNG (1858–1933), Architect

Xerox copy of an album of press-cuttings
relating to buildings designed by G P K
Young, including: restoration of St John's
Church, Perth; reconstruction of Fettercairn
Parish Church; Northern District School,
Perth; Perth Fever Hospital; temporary
building for Free Church Assembly, Inverness,
etc. *c.*1890–1910.
Original in possession of Miss Elsie Young.

INDEX

Only those subjects mentioned in the catalogue are included in the index.

HMSO

HMSO publications are available from:

HMSO Bookshops

71 Lothian Road, Edinburgh, EH3 9AZ   031-228 4181
49 High Holborn, London, WC1V 6HB   071-873 0011 (Counter service only)
258 Broad Street, Birmingham, B1 2HE   021-643 3740
Southey House, 33 Wine Street, Bristol BS1 2BQ   (0272) 264306
9-21 Princess Street, Manchester, M60 8AS   061-834 7201
80 Chichester Street, Belfast BT1 4JY   (0232) 238451

HMSO Publications Centre

(Mail and telephone orders only)
PO Box 276, London, SW8 5DT
Telephone orders 071-873 9090
General enquiries 071-873 0011
(queuing system in operation for both numbers)

HMSO's Accredited Agents
(see Yellow Pages)

And through good booksellers